OXFORD

FLASHLIGHT

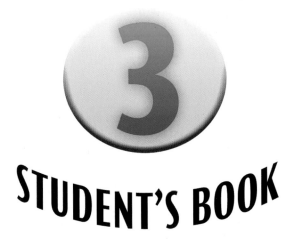

3

STUDENT'S BOOK

Paul A Davies & Tim Falla

FLASHLIGHT CONTENTS

Everyday English	Grammar 2	Reading and Writing	Focus on the World
• Talking about school	• Revision: *there's / there are*		
• Talking about plans	• *some* and *any* • *must / mustn't*	• My worst day at school • Sequencing words: *before, then, after, later* • A really bad day	• Six days that changed the world
• Talking about likes and dislikes	• Question words • Adverbs of frequency • Object pronouns	• My best friend • Capital letters and punctuation • Describing a friend	• Australia
• Describing people	• Present continuous with future meaning • *should / shouldn't*	• Band fact-file • Word order • Linkin Park	• Music and dance
• Giving opinions	• Superlative adjectives	• Malcolm in the middle • *because* • My favourite TV programme	• Cinema
• Talking about your weekend	• Past simple negative and interrogative • *could / couldn't*	• William Shakespeare • Using notes • A biography of Frida Kahlo	• Madame Tussaud

Introduction

WHAT'S IN THIS UNIT?

- Describing people
- Revision of vocabulary from Book 2: school subjects, food and drink
- Revision: *be* present simple
- Revision: *have got*
- Revision: *there's / there are*
- Talking about school

SARAH'S WORLD

1 🎧 Read and listen. Find Sarah, Kelly and Luke in the photos.

1 Hi! My name's Sarah Portland. I'm fourteen years old and I've got long, fair hair and blue eyes. I'm from Notting Hill - that's in London. Notting Hill is OK. There are shops and cafés, and there's a great cinema. But there isn't a swimming pool.

2 I haven't got any sisters, but I've got a brother. His name's Luke. He's eight years old. He's got short, fair hair and glasses. He's annoying sometimes, but he's OK really. His favourite food is chicken and chips.

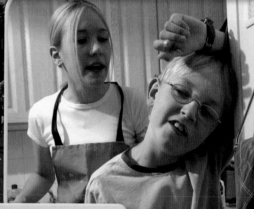

3 My best friend is Kelly Sampson. She's fifteen years old and she's got long, dark hair and brown eyes. We're in the same class at St Philip's Secondary School. Her favourite subjects are art and English. My favourite subject is history. Kelly hasn't got any brothers or sisters, but she's got a lot of friends.

2 Answer the questions.

1 How old is Sarah?
2 Where's she from?
3 Has she got any brothers or sisters?
4 How old is Luke?
5 Are Sarah and Kelly in different classes?
6 What are Kelly's favourite subjects?
7 How many brothers and sisters has she got?

3 MAPS Find London on the map on page 66.

4 REAL ENGLISH Who says these expressions? What do they mean?

1 Notting Hill is OK.

2 He's annoying sometimes.

3 His favourite food is chicken and chips.

5 Introduce yourself to the class.

Hi. My name's ...

I'm ... years old.

My favourite subjects are ... and ...

My favourite food is ...

VOCABULARY

Describing people

1 Match the descriptions with Sarah, Luke and Kelly.

1 short, fair hair and glasses
2 long, dark hair and brown eyes
3 long, fair hair and blue eyes

2 Describe the people in the photos. Use the words in the box to help you.

> **Height**
> tall / short / medium height
> **Hair**
> long / short   dark / fair   straight / curly
> **Eyes**
> brown / blue / green / grey
> **Other things**
> glasses / a beard / a moustache

John 1m 98cm

Adama 1m 60cm

Ho 1m 45cm

Vanessa 1m 75cm

> John is very tall. He's got long ...

3 Describe people in your class.

> Maria is medium height. She's got short, dark hair and brown eyes.

Revision: school subjects

4 Find three school subjects on page 4.

5 Complete the labels.

1 c _ _ _ _ _ _ _
   s _ _ _ _ _ _

2 g _ _ _ _ _ _ _ _

3 s _ _ _ _ _ _

4 F _ _ _ _ _

5 _ _

6 m _ _ _ _

7 m _ _ _ _

6 Which of the school subjects in exercises 4 and 5 do you study?

Revision: food and drink

7 Put the words in the correct column.

> apples   beer   chocolate   cheese   coffee
> crisps   lemonade   milk   orange juice
> pizza

Food	Drink

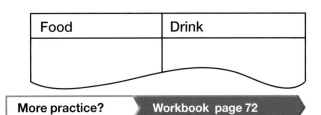

More practice?   Workbook page 72

GRAMMAR 1

Revision: *be* present simple

1 Copy and complete the table.

Affirmative	I am you … he …
	we … you … they …
Negative	I … you aren't she …
	we … you … they …
Interrogative	Am I? … you? … it?
	… we? … you? … they?

2 Write true sentences. Use the affirmative or negative of *be*.

I / 16 years old
I'm not 16 years old.

1 I / from Argentina
2 My mum / a teacher
3 We / in the classroom
4 My friends / English
5 It / very hot today
6 Raúl / my favourite footballer

Watch out!

We use *be* not *have got* in these expressions.
I've got hungry. ✗
I'm hungry. ✔
I've got 13 years old. ✗
I'm 13 years old. ✔

3 Put the words in the correct order to make questions. Then write true short answers.

Hernán Crespo / Chile / from / is ?
Is Hernán Crespo from Chile?
No, he isn't.

1 your / is / long / hair ?
2 you / a maths lesson / are / in ?
3 your best friend / is / at home ?
4 hungry / are / you ?
5 Tuesday / it / is / today ?
6 your / Venus and Serena Williams / are / favourite tennis players ?

Revision: *have got*

4 Copy and complete the table.

Affirmative
I / you / we / they have got   dark hair. he / she / it (1)……

Negative
I / you / we / they (2)……   dark hair. he / she / it hasn't got

Interrogative
have I / you / we / they got dark hair? (3)……he / she / it (4)……

5 Ask and answer about these things. Which things have you both got?

Have you got a CD player?

Yes, I have. / No, I haven't.

1 a CD player
2 a dog
3 a guitar
4 a computer
5 a bike
6 a sister
7 blue eyes
8 a mobile phone

6 Tell the class about your partner.

Maria hasn't got a CD player.

She's got …

More practice?	Workbook pages 73–74

Talking about school

1 Label the picture of the school. use the words in the box.

> canteen classroom computer room
> gym hall library playground
> teacher's room

2 🎧 Listen. Where are the people? Number the places in the order you hear them.

a computer room
b teacher's room
c canteen
d gym
e library

3 Match the questions and answers.

1 Which school are you at?
2 Which class are you in?
3 How many students are there in your class?
4 What subjects do you do?
5 What's your favourite subject?
6 What time does school start?
7 What time does school finish?
8 Are you a member of any school clubs?

a I'm in class 4B.
b At quarter to nine.
c English, science, history, geography, art and PE.
d At four o'clock.
e I'm at Stowhill Secondary School.
f Science.
g 29.
h Yes, I'm a member of the football club.

4 🎧 Listen to Mandy doing a survey. She writes some of the answers incorrectly. Correct the false information.

School survey

Name: Mark

1 Newport Secondary School
2 4B
3 28 students
4 maths, science, history, geography, PE, art
5 history
6 9.00
7 3.45
8 chess and karate

5 Ask and answer the questions in the survey.

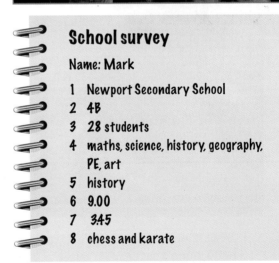

> Which school are you at?

> I'm at ...

More practice?	Workbook page 75

GRAMMAR 2

Revision: *there's / there are*

1 Copy and complete the table. Use *is*, *isn't*, *are* and *aren't*.

	Affirmative	Negative	Interrogative
Singular	There (1) ...... a bike.	There (3) ...... a bike.	(5) ...... there a bike? Yes, there is. / No, there isn't.
Plural	There (2) ...... two bikes.	There (4) ...... any bikes.	(6) ...... there any bikes? Yes, there are. / No, there aren't.

> **Take note!**
>
> We use *any* before plural nouns in negative and interrogative sentences.
> There aren't **any** biscuits.
> Are there **any** biscuits?

2 Look at the photo of Emily's bedroom and write sentences. Use *There's* or *There are* and the correct number.

poster
There's one poster.

1 bag
2 tennis balls
3 tennis rackets
4 CD player
5 chairs
6 volleyball

3 Write sentences using *There isn't* or *There aren't*.

1 any books
2 a computer
3 a table
4 any biscuits
5 a guitar
6 any photos

4 Look at the photo of Alex's bedroom. Complete the questions. Use *Is there* or *Are there*.

1 ...... any posters?
2 ...... a table?
3 ...... any CDs?
4 ...... a computer?
5 ...... any books?
6 ...... a CD player?

5 In pairs, ask and answer the questions in exercise 4.

> Are there any posters?

> No, there aren't.

Communicate!

Write five sentences about things in your bedroom. Compare with a partner.
There's a table in my bedroom.
There isn't a computer.

More practice?	Workbook pages 73–74

1 Good Days, Bad Days

WHAT'S IN THIS UNIT?

- Adjectives to describe feelings
- Places in town
- Recognising parts of speech
- Past simple affirmative (regular verbs)
- *some* and *any*
- *going to*
- *must / mustn't*
- Talking about plans
- Sequencing words: *then, later, after, before*

VOCABULARY

Adjectives to describe feelings

1 🎧 Listen and repeat the adjectives in the box. What do they mean?

> annoyed disappointed embarrassed
> excited frightened jealous nervous
> pleased surprised

2 Choose the correct adjective.

1 I watched a horror film.
   I was **frightened / embarrassed**.
2 I failed my maths exam.
   I was **jealous / disappointed**.
3 I missed the bus.
   I was **frightened / annoyed**.
4 My teacher liked my English essay.
   I was **surprised / nervous**.
5 My dad danced at my birthday party.
   I was really **frightened / embarrassed**.
6 I was **excited / nervous** before the exam, but it was OK.

3 Talk about the people in the photos. Use the adjectives from exercise 1.

> I think he looks …   I don't think he looks …

4 Complete the sentences with your own ideas.

1 I feel annoyed when …
2 I feel nervous when …
3 I feel pleased when …
4 I feel excited when …

More practice? **Workbook page 76**

SARAH'S STORY

When Harry met Sarah

1 Last Saturday, the weather was terrible. In fact, it rained all the time. In the morning, Kelly and I walked around the shopping centre and looked at the shops. In the afternoon, we were bored. There weren't any good films on at the cinema, so we visited the Internet café in town …

Are there any interesting people in the chat-room?

There's only one other person – a boy, I think.

What's his name?

We aren't using our real names. He's "MetalHead" and I'm "Dreamer".

Kelly

2

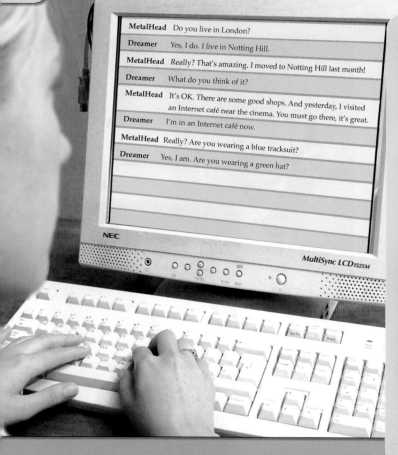

MetalHead	Do you live in London?
Dreamer	Yes, I do. I live in Notting Hill.
MetalHead	Really? That's amazing. I moved to Notting Hill last month!
Dreamer	What do you think of it?
MetalHead	It's OK. There are some good shops. And yesterday, I visited an Internet café near the cinema. You must go there, it's great.
Dreamer	I'm in an Internet café now.
MetalHead	Really? Are you wearing a blue tracksuit?
Dreamer	Yes, I am. Are you wearing a green hat?

NEC   MultiSync LCD1525M

Hi! I'm Harry. Nice to meet you.

Hello. I'm Sarah.

This is weird.

3 What a coincidence! We were in the same Internet café! Kelly was really surprised. My first thought was: it's fate - Harry and I are going to be good friends …

1 🎧 Read and listen to Sarah's story. Why is Kelly surprised at the end?

a) Sarah and Harry aren't using their real names.

b) Harry is wearing a green hat and Sarah is wearing a blue tracksuit.

c) Sarah meets Harry online but he's also in the same Internet café.

2 Are these sentences true or false? Correct the false ones.

1 The weather was OK last Saturday.

2 Kelly and Sarah looked at the shops in the morning.

3 There were some good films on at the cinema.

4 Kelly and Sarah visited the Internet café in the afternoon.

5 "MetalHead" was really Kelly.

6 Harry moved to Notting Hill yesterday.

3 REAL ENGLISH Who says these expressions? What do they mean?

1 What do you think of it?

2 What a coincidence!

3 Nice to meet you!

4 This is weird!

Teen focus

Using computers
Read what Harry says about computers.
Do you use computers?

I love using computers. I've got a new computer at home and I play lots of games on it. There's a good Internet café in town, and I sometimes go there and visit chat rooms. We also use computers at school.

Word check Places in town

4 In the story, find the places in town where you can do these things.

1 visit a lot of different shops

2 watch a film

3 have food and drink, and use a computer

5 Match the places (1–5) with the things you can do there (a–e).

1 supermarket
2 library
3 post office
4 school
5 bus stop

a read books
b have lessons
c buy food
d catch a bus
e buy stamps

6 Think of examples in your own town of the places in exercises 4 and 5. Where are they?

There's a supermarket near our school. It's on Avenida ...

| More practice? | Workbook page 76 |

Study skills

Recognizing parts of speech

7 Match the groups of words (1–4) with the parts of speech (a–d).

1 play   go   listen   be

2 tall   short   easy   difficult

3 they   it   us   me

4 friend   school   notebook   music

a nouns

b verbs

c pronouns

d adjectives

8 Find three more words of each part of speech in the story. Add them to the correct group in exercise 7.

GRAMMAR 1

Past simple affirmative (regular verbs)

1 Copy and complete the table.

Spelling: past simple affirmative		
Normal		
watch	+ -ed	→ watched
listen	+ -ed	→ (1) ......
Final -e		
live	+ -d	→ lived
dance	+ -d	→ (2) ......
Final consonant + -y		
worry	-y + -ied	→ worried
study	-y + -ied	→ (3) ......
Short vowel + consonant		
stop	double consonant + -ed	→ stopped
chat		→ (4) ......

> **Take note!**
>
> The past simple form doesn't change:
> I worked, she worked, they worked

2 Complete the sentences. Use the past simple affirmative of the verbs in the box. Which sentences are true for you?

> ask   study   visit   wash   watch

1 My dad .... English at school.
2 I ...... a foreign country last year.
3 My best friend ...... TV last night.
4 I ...... my hair this morning.
5 My teacher ...... me a difficult question in the last lesson.

Pronunciation /d/ /t/ and /ɪd/

3 🎧 Listen. Pay attention to the different endings.

A /d/ / /t/	lived, listened, watched, looked
B /ɪd/	started, hated

4 🎧 Listen. Write A or B.

1	wanted	3	cooked	5	loved
2	arrived	4	visited	6	stopped

going to

5 Complete the chart. Use the correct form of the verb *be*.

Affirmative
I'm going to see a film.
We (1) ...... going to see a film.
Negative
He (2) ...... going to see a film.
You (3) ...... going to see a film.
Interrogative
(4)...... she going to see a film?
(5)...... they going to see a film?

6 Complete the text. Use the correct form of *going to* and the verbs in the box.

> do   buy   go   go out   have   play   watch

My plans for next Saturday
On Saturday morning my sister Mei and I are going to go shopping. I (1) ...... some new trainers.
In the afternoon Mei (2) ...... volleyball. She's in the school team and it's an important match, so my parents and I (3) ...... the match.
In the evening I (4) ...... my homework, then I (5) ...... with my friend Tom. We (6) ...... a burger and chips.

7 Write true sentences about your plans for next Saturday. Use *going to*, affirmative or negative and the phrases in the box.

> go to a disco   do sport   visit
> my grandparents   have a party   do
> my homework   go to the cinema
> go shopping   go out with my friends

I'm (not) going to go to a disco.

More practice?   Workbook pages 77–78

Dialogue

1 🎧 Read and listen. Answer the questions.

    1 What does Kelly plan to do this weekend?
    2 Do Kelly's parents know about her plans?

TALKING ABOUT PLANS

Kelly	Have you got any plans for this weekend?
Sarah	No, I haven't. Why?
Kelly	I'm going to invite some friends around for a sleep-over. Can you come?
Sarah	Yes, I can. That sounds really good!
Kelly	We're going to watch horror films and eat pizzas.
Sarah	Do your parents mind?
Kelly	They don't know about it yet. I'm going to tell them about it tonight.
Sarah	Good luck!

2 **REAL ENGLISH** 🎧 Listen and repeat these expressions from the dialogue.

    1 a sleep-over
    2 That sounds really good!
    3 Do your parents mind?
    4 Good luck!

3 Practise reading the dialogue.

4 Write your own dialogue. Choose from these plans.

> have a party – invite all my friends
> go to a pop concert – stay with a friend
> go shopping – get a new mobile phone

A: Have you got any plans for this weekend?
B: No, I haven't. Why?

5 Act out your dialogue in class.

More practice?   Workbook page 79

Listening

6 🎧 Listen to Kelly and her mum. Which of these does her mum agree to?

    a) having a sleep-over
    b) eating pizzas
    c) watching horror films

7 🎧 Listen again. Answer the questions.

    1 Where is Kelly's mum going to do the shopping?
    2 What does Kelly ask her mum to buy?
    3 How many friends does Kelly want at the sleep-over?
    4 How many friends does Kelly's mum agree to?
    5 When is Kelly's birthday?
    6 How old is she going to be?
    7 What does Kelly agree to watch?

GRAMMAR 2

some and any

1 Study the examples and complete the rules.

Affirmative
There's some pasta. There are some oranges.
Negative
There isn't any pasta. There aren't any oranges.
Interrogative
Is there any pasta? Are there any oranges?

1 We use …… in affirmative sentences.
2 We use …… in negative sentences and questions.

2 🎧 Complete the conversation. Use *some* and *any*. Then listen and check.

Neil I'm hungry. Are there any biscuits?
Mum No, there aren't (1) …… biscuits. But we've got (2) …… chocolate cake.
Neil I don't like chocolate cake. Can I have a sandwich?
Mum There isn't (3) …… bread.
Neil Is there (4) …… fruit?
Mum Yes, there are (5) …… apples.
Neil Are there (6) …… bananas?
Mum Yes, there are (7) …… bananas on the kitchen table.

More practice?	Workbook pages 77–78

must / mustn't

3 Complete the examples with *must* and *mustn't*. Then answer the questions.

Affirmative
I must go to bed. She …… do her homework.
Negative
We …… eat in class. He mustn't go to bed late. (full form: must not)

1 Do we use *to* after *must/mustn't*?
2 Is the third person singular form different?
3 What is the full form of *mustn't*?

4 Complete the sentences with *must* or *mustn't*.

It's a fantastic CD. You must listen to it.
1 You …… tell George about the party. It's a secret!
2 We …… eat or drink in class.
3 I …… go home now. It's very late.
4 We haven't got any milk. We …… get some from the shop.
5 It's grandad's birthday on Sunday. You …… forget to send him a card.

5 Write sentences with *must* and the phrases in the box.

get a passport	practise every day
go to bed early	put on some sun cream
go to the shoe shop	go to the bank

I need some new trainers.
You must go to the shoe shop.
1 I haven't got any money.
2 I'm going to visit the USA next summer.
3 I want to be a professional footballer.
4 I'm going to go to the beach.
5 I've got an exam tomorrow.

Communicate!

Write four sentences about things that you must do this weekend. Compare with a partner.
I must help my mum with the cooking.

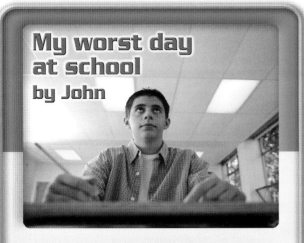

My worst day at school
by John

The day started really badly. In the morning, I missed the bus, so I walked to school instead. Then it started to rain! I arrived late and my teacher was a bit annoyed. The lesson before lunch was maths. My friend Tom copied all my answers. It wasn't my fault, but the teacher was angry with me! I was very upset.

After lunch, the history teacher asked me a question about Christopher Columbus. I answered, 'Columbus discovered America in 1942'. Everyone laughed. I was really embarrassed.

In the evening, I watched my favourite football team on TV. They played really badly. The other team scored six goals! Later in the evening I argued with my mum. It was a terrible day!

Reading

1 🎧 Read about John's worst day at school. Find these time expressions in the model text. What do they mean?

before   Then   after   When   Later

2 Are the sentences true or false? Correct the false ones.

1 John walked to school because the bus was late.
2 John copied Tom's maths answers.
3 John's answer in the history lesson was incorrect.
4 John was annoyed when everyone laughed.
5 John's favourite football team scored six goals.
6 John argued with his dad.

Writing   Sequencing words

3 Choose the correct word.

1 It started to rain **before** / **then** we arrived at the bus stop.
2 The first lesson **later** / **after** lunch was maths.
3 I watched TV. **Then** / **After** I listened to music.
4 **Later** / **Before** dad cooked dinner, he washed the car.
5 **After** / **Later** that evening I watched a film.

4 Imagine a really bad day. Note down three bad things that happened. Use the ideas in the box to help you.

watched an awful terrible video/DVD
watched a terrible match on TV
argued with my friend / my parents
missed the bus / train
arrived late
it rained a lot

5 Use your notes to write a text. Use some of the expressions in exercise 1.

Paragraph 1
My ...... day at school was about ...... ago.
In the morning ... Then ...
Paragraph 2
After lunch ...
Paragraph 3
In the evening ... Later ...

| More practice? | Workbook pages 79–80 |

1 🎧 **Test your general knowledge. Complete the texts with the dates.**

| 26th January 1926 | 20th July 1969 | 6th August 1991 |
| 11th September 2001 | 4th April 1968 | 6th August 1945 |

Six days that changed the world

On (1)......, in a small laboratory in London, Scottish engineer John Logie Baird transmitted the first television pictures.

The Americans dropped an atomic bomb on Hiroshima, Japan on (2)...... . About 150,000 people died. Nine days later, Japan surrendered and the Second World War ended.

On (3)...... James Earl Ray assassinated Martin Luther King in Memphis. King wanted equal rights for blacks in the southern states of the USA.

Apollo 11 landed on the moon on (4)...... . Neil Armstrong and Buzz Aldrin climbed out of the lunar module and walked on the moon.

On (5)...... Tim Berners Lee invented the worldwide web. He wanted to share information on the internet with other scientists.

On (6)...... terrorists hijacked planes from Boston Airport and crashed them into the World Trade Centre in New York and the Pentagon in Washington. Over 3,000 people died, and the "War on Terror" started.

2 MAPS Find or mark the cities mentioned in exercise 1 on the maps on pages 66, 67 and 68-9.

3 Complete these sentences with information from the text.

1 John Logie Baird was from ....
2 About ...... people died in Hiroshima.
3 Martin Luther King wanted equal rights for ....
4 Neil Armstrong and ...... walked on the moon.
5 Over ...... people died when terrorists attacked the World Trade Centre.

4 What's your opinion? Put the six days in order of importance.

5 Work with a partner. Think of other days that changed the world.

Song and Reading File page 57.

OXFORD

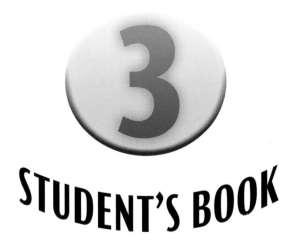

3

STUDENT'S BOOK

Paul A Davies & Tim Falla

FLASHLIGHT CONTENTS

VOCABULARY

WHAT'S IN THIS UNIT?

- Activities
- Sports
- Present simple
- Question words
- Adverbs of frequency
- Object pronouns
- Talking about likes and dislikes
- Capital letters and punctuation

Activities

1 🎧 Match the words with the pictures. Then listen and repeat.

listen to music   play volleyball   go to the cinema   play computer games
read magazines   surf the Internet   meet friends   go shopping

2 🎧 Listen. What do Kelly, David and Julia do at the weekend? Which activities do they do?

Kelly	David	Julia
1 ……	1 ……	1 ……
2 ……	2 ……	2 ……

3 What about you? Put the activities from exercise 1 into three groups.

I often do it	
I sometimes do it	
I never do it	

More practice?   **Workbook page 81**

At the bowling alley

Kelly

Harry

1 It's Sunday afternoon and Harry wants to go bowling with me and Kelly. It's his favourite hobby. It isn't mine! I like music and shopping. Kelly is interested in music and magazines. She doesn't like bowling, but she's a good friend …

I can't go without you. I don't know Harry very well. Please come!

I never go bowling … but OK. Just for you!

2 Harry loves sport. He plays football and tennis at school, and he often goes weight-training at the weekend. Kelly sometimes does aerobics, but she isn't really interested in sport. She's interested in clothes …

I can't wear those shoes! They're horrible!

You must.

Everybody wears them here.

3 Kelly doesn't usually like bowling, but she's enjoying it now. Why? Because she's winning!

Great! Ten points– again!

I never get ten points.

Don't worry.

1 🎧 **Read and listen. Why does Kelly change her opinion about bowling?**

1 Because she likes the shoes.
2 Because it's boring.
3 Because she's winning.

2 Answer the questions.

1 Who wants to go bowling?
2 Who likes shopping?
3 What sports does Harry play at school?
4 When does Harry go weight-training?
5 What is Kelly's opinion of the shoes at the bowling alley?
6 Who gets ten points?

3 REAL ENGLISH Who says these expressions? What do they mean?

1 Please come!

2 Just for you.

3 Great!

4 Don't worry.

Teen focus

Music
Read what Sarah says about music. Then give your opinion about music.

I like lots of different kinds of music and I listen to the radio every day. My favourite kind of music is dance music. I don't really like heavy metal.

Word check Sports

4 How many sports can you find in the story? Add them to the chart.

play (ball games)	go (-*ing*)	do (other sports)
basketball	skiing	gymnastics
(1) ……	(2) ……	(3) ……

5 Add these sports to the chart in exercise 4. Can you add any others?

cycling   karate   surfing

6 In pairs, ask and answer about sports.

1 Which sports do you like?
2 Which sports don't you like?
3 Which sports are you good at?

More practice?   Workbook page 81

Study skills

Recording new vocabulary

7 Look at the different ways of recording new vocabulary. Which ones do you use?

1 translation
  weight-training = entrenamiento con pesos
2 definition
  weight-training = lifting weights to get fit
3 picture
  weight-training =

4 example
  weight-training: I go weight-training at the gym to get fit.

8 Record these words from the story in two different ways.

1 shopping
2 magazines
3 shoes

Present simple

1 Copy and complete the table.

Affirmative	Negative	Interrogative
I play	I **(3)** ...... play	Do I play ?
you play	you don't play	Do you play ?
he **(1)**	he doesn't play	Does he play ?
she plays	she doesn't play	**(5)** ...... she play ?
it plays	it **(4)** ......play	Does it play ?
we play	we don't play	Do we play ?
you **(2)**	you don't play	Do you play ?
they play	they don't play	**(6)** ...... they play ?
	Full forms I don't play = I do not play he doesn't play = he does not play	**Short answers** Yes, I do. / No, I don't. Yes, she does. / No, she doesn't.

2 Complete the sentences with the present simple affirmative of the verbs in the box.

> finish go meet ~~play~~ study surf watch

My best friend **plays** computer games.

1 Thomas and I ...... to the cinema at weekends.
2 My sister ...... her friends in the café.
3 Martin and Kate ...... music at school.
4 Emma ...... basketball on TV.
5 I ...... the Internet in the evenings.
6 School ...... at four o'clock.

3 Make the sentences in exercise 2 negative.

My best friend doesn't play computer games.

4 Put the words in the correct order to make questions. Then write true answers.

you and your friends / play / do / football
Do you and your friends play football?
Yes, we do. / No, we don't.

1 surf / does / your / the Internet / best friend ?
2 your teacher / lunch / have / at school / does ?
3 listen / at home / you / to / do / music ?
4 the cinema / you and your friends / go / to / do / at weekends ?
5 computer games / you / do / play ?
6 go / do / shopping / after school / you ?

5 Complete the email. Use the present simple affirmative, negative and interrogative.

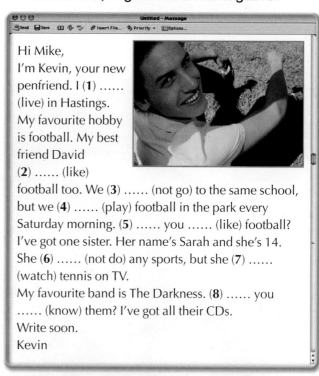

Untitled - Message

Hi Mike,
I'm Kevin, your new penfriend. I **(1)** ...... (live) in Hastings. My favourite hobby is football. My best friend David **(2)** ...... (like) football too. We **(3)** ...... (not go) to the same school, but we **(4)** ...... (play) football in the park every Saturday morning. **(5)** ...... you ...... (like) football? I've got one sister. Her name's Sarah and she's 14. She **(6)** ...... (not do) any sports, but she **(7)** ...... (watch) tennis on TV. My favourite band is The Darkness. **(8)** ...... you ...... (know) them? I've got all their CDs.
Write soon.
Kevin

Communicate!

Ask your partner three questions about what they do at the weekend.
Do you watch TV?

More practice?	Workbook pages 82–83

Dialogue

1 🎧 **Read and listen. Complete the dialogue with the words in the box.**

> music   cool   like   new   really

TALKING ABOUT LIKES AND DISLIKES

Hannah What CD is this, Emily?

Emily It's the **(1)** ...... Blue CD.

Hannah I can't stand Blue!

Emily What **(2)** ...... do you like?

Hannah Linkin Park.

Emily What about Nickelback? Do you **(3)** ...... them?

Hannah They're fantastic. The guitarist is really **(4)** ....

Emily Yeah, I **(5)** ...... like them, too.

2 🎧 **Listen and repeat the phrases from the dialogue.**

1 I can't stand Blue!

2 What music do you like?

3 What about Nickelback?

3 **Practise reading the dialogue.**

4 **Write your own dialogue. Use music that you like.**

A: What CD ... ?

B: It's the new ...

A: I can't ...

B: What music ... ?

A: ...

B: What about ... ? Do ... ?

A: They're ...

B: Yeah, I ...

5 **Act out your dialogue.**

> What CD ... ?

> It's the new ...

More practice?	Workbook page 84

Listening

6 🎧 **Listen to Joe and Emily. Which two teams are playing?**

a) Newcastle United   c) Manchester United

b) Tottenham   d) Leeds United

7 🎧 **Listen again. Are the sentences true or false? Correct the false sentences.**

1 The football match is Manchester United v Tottenham.

2 Tottenham are winning 3–1.

3 Joe likes Manchester United.

4 They both like Van Nistelrooy.

5 Van Nistelrooy scores a goal.

6 Emily thinks Manchester United are boring.

7 Joe's favourite player is Robbie Keane.

GRAMMAR 2

Question words

1 Read the question words.

Who? Where? When? Why? How often? What?

2 Complete the questions. Use the question words from exercise 1.

How often do you go to the cinema?
1 ...... is your favourite film star?
2 ...... do you like him/her?
3 ...... do you meet your friends at weekends – at home or in town?
4 ...... is your favourite sport?
5 ...... do you do your homework – before or after school?

3 In pairs, ask and answer the questions in exercise 2.

> How often do you go to the cinema?

> About once a month.

Adverbs of frequency

4 Copy and complete the chart. Use *often*, *sometimes* and *usually*.

100% ⟶ 0%
always (1) ...... (2) ...... (3) ...... hardly ever never

Take note!

Adverbs of frequency go **before** most verbs in the present simple.
I **always** watch TV in the evening.

They go **after** the verb *be*.
My friend is **often** late for school.

5 Write sentences about what these friends do at weekends.

Joey / go to the cinema (sometimes)
Joey sometimes goes to the cinema.
1 Joey and Ross / watch TV (often)
2 Phoebe / do athletics (never)
3 Ross / cook (hardly ever)
4 Joey / be hungry (always)
5 they / see Chandler and Monica every day (usually)
6 Rachel / read fashion magazines (sometimes)

Object pronouns

6 Study the information. Which object pronouns are the same as the subject pronouns?

Take note!

subject	object	subject	object
I	me	we	us
you	you	you	you
he	him	they	them
she	her		
it	it		

More practice? Workbook pages 82–83

Pronunciation Word stress

7 🎧 Listen and repeat. Pay attention to the word stress.

1 volleyball 3 computer 5 magazine
2 cinema 4 exciting 6 afternoon

My best friend

My best friend is Sue Walker. She's thirteen years old and her birthday is on 1st March. She's got two brothers. Their names are Mark and Sam. She's got a lot of pets. She's got a dog, a mouse, a cat, two rabbits and some fish.

Sue is tall and thin. She's got fair hair and blue eyes.

Sue and I go to the same school. It's called Langdale Comprehensive. We're in the same class. Sue's favourite subjects are science and biology.

Sue's favourite sport is tennis. We sometimes play tennis together at the weekend. Her favourite players are Serena Williams and Lleyton Hewitt. Sue likes films too. We don't go to the cinema very often, but we watch DVDs at her house.

Reading

1 Look at the photo of Sue. What animals does she like?

2 🎧 Read the text. Answer the questions.

   1 How many brothers has she got?
   2 What pets has she got?
   3 What colour is her hair?
   4 What are her favourite subjects?
   5 Who are her favourite tennis players?
   6 Where do they watch DVDs?

Writing Capital letters and punctuation

3 Study the rules.

> **We use capital letters for:**
>
> - the start of a sentence
> - the first person pronoun, '*I*'
> - people, places and nationalities (*Sue*, *Madrid*, *American*)
> - days and months
>
> **Punctuation marks**
>
> - full stop   **.**
> - comma   **,**
> - question mark   **?**
> - exclamation mark   **!**
> - apostrophe   **'**

4 Add capital letters and punctuation to the sentences.

   1 my best friends name is sue
   2 im tom and im from new york
   3 whats your favourite sport
   4 i play volleyball on mondays wednesdays and thursdays
   5 my parents best friends are american
   6 dont run

5 Write a text about your best friend. Use the writing plan to help you.

> **Paragraph 1**
> My best friend is …
> He's/She's … years old.
> His/Her birthday is on …
> He's/She's got … (brothers? sisters? pets?)
> **Paragraph 2**
> He's/She's tall/short.
> He's/She's got … (hair? eyes?)
> **Paragraph 3**
> … and I go to …
> His/Her favourite subject is …
> **Paragraph 4**
> He/She likes …
> He/She likes/plays … (sports?)

| More practice? | Workbook pages 84–85 |

FOCUS ON THE WORLD

1 🎧 Read the texts (1–5) and match them to the headings (a–e).

a) Sport   d) Aborigines

b) Introduction   e) Important cities

c) Famous Australians

AUSTRALIA

1 Australia is a very big country. It's 4,000 kilometres from east to west, but it has a population of only 20 million.

2 Sydney, Melbourne, Perth and Brisbane are important cities in Australia. They're all next to the sea. The capital of Australia is Canberra.

3 The Aborigines are the original inhabitants of Australia. At Aborigine festivals, they sing, dance and play the didgeridoo, a traditional instrument.

4 Australians love sport. Team sports are very popular – for example, cricket and rugby. A lot of people go swimming, surfing and cycling, too.

2 Answer the questions.

1 What is the population of Australia?

2 What is the capital of Australia?

3 What is a didgeridoo?

4 Which team sports are popular in Australia?

5 Which two friends and famous film stars are Australian?

3 **MAPS** Find out where the cities in the text are. Find or mark them on the map on pages 68–9.

5 Film stars Nicole Kidman and Russell Crowe are from Australia – and they're good friends too. Australian TV programmes are popular in many other countries. Sometimes the actors become famous – Kylie Minogue, for example.

Song and Reading File page 57.

Music

WHAT'S IN THIS UNIT?

- Instruments and musicians
- Clothes
- Present continuous
- Present continuous with future meaning
- *should / shouldn't*
- Describing people
- Word order

VOCABULARY

Instruments and musicians

1 🎧 Match the words with the instruments. Then listen and repeat.

bass guitar cello drums guitar keyboard piano saxophone trumpet violin

2 🎧 Listen and repeat the musicians. Then write sentences.

guitarist saxophonist violinist cellist pianist
keyboard player bass guitarist trumpeter drummer

A guitarist plays the guitar.
A saxophonist plays ...

3 🎧 Listen and identify the instruments.

1 trumpet   2 ...

| More practice? | Workbook page 86 |

KELLY'S STORY

An embarrassing mistake

1 Harry is having a party at his house next Saturday. Sarah can't go. She's really disappointed.

Harry

Sarah

That's a shame. What are you doing next Saturday?

I'm visiting my cousins in Brighton.

A party! Hmm. I should buy some new clothes …

2 At the party, everybody is dancing and chatting. Harry's friends are really nice, and the food is great. I'm wearing a new jacket with a white top, black jeans and trainers. I look cool! The only problem is the music! It's all heavy metal. I hate heavy metal! I want to go home, but I don't want to offend Harry …

Listen to this CD. He's a great drummer! Oh! Are you leaving?

I'm sorry. I'm having a great time, but I don't feel well.

3 When I get home, I send a text to Sarah.

Did U have fun? Left party early 2nite because music was terrible! :-((CU soon K

4 The reply is from Harry, not from Kelly. Oh no! I texted the wrong person! This is so embarrassing …

Sorry about music. My fault. I should buy some new CDs! CU soon H

26 Unit 3

1 🎧 Read and listen. Are the sentences true or false? Correct the false sentences.

1 Sarah can't go to the party because she's visiting her grandparents.
2 Kelly likes the music at the party.
3 Kelly sends a text to Harry.

2 Answer the questions.

1 Where is Harry having his party?
2 What is Kelly wearing at the party?
3 Why does Kelly want to go home?
4 What does Kelly tell Harry?
5 Why is Kelly embarrassed?

3 **REAL ENGLISH** Who says these expressions? What do they mean?

1 That's a shame.

2 I look cool.

3 Are you leaving?

4 My fault.

Teen focus

Text messages
Read what Kelly says about text messages. Then say how *you* use them.

I send about twenty text messages every day. They're usually very short - Hi, I'm on the bus. Where R U? - or something like that

Word check   Clothes

4 Look at the story. What are Harry, Kelly and Sarah wearing? Use the words in the box.

> jeans   hat   trousers   jacket   T-shirt
> shirt   sweatshirt   tie   jumper

Sarah in photo 1. *She's wearing a white shirt and a green jumper.*

1 Harry in photo 1
2 Kelly in photo 1
3 Kelly in photo 2
4 Harry in photo 2

5 Ask and answer about people in your class.

What's David wearing?

A T-shirt, tracksuit bottoms and trainers.

More practice?   Workbook page 86

Study skills

Learning vocabulary

6 Read what the students say about learning vocabulary. Who has the best method, in your opinion? What method do you use?

Hiroko I don't learn vocabulary at home, but I try to remember the new words that I see when I'm in class.

Carlos I look at my book at home and try to remember new words. Sometimes it works!

Katya I write down ten new words each week and try to remember them. I sometimes look at them when I'm on the bus.

Farhani I learn new words with a friend. We try to remember them, then we test each other.

7 Choose five words from the story and learn them.

Present continuous

1 Copy and complete the table. What are the full forms of the present continuous?

Affirmative	Negative	Interrogative
I'm singing	I (3) …… singing	Am I singing ?
you (1) …… singing	you aren't singing	Are you singing ?
he's singing	he isn't singing	(6) …… he singing ?
she's singing	she isn't singing	Is she singing ?
it's singing	it (4) …… singing	Is it singing ?
we (2) …… singing	we aren't singing	Are we singing ?
you're singing	you aren't singing	(7) …… you singing ?
they're singing	they (5) …… singing	Are they singing ?
We use the present continuous for actions which are happening now.		**Short answers** Yes, I am. / No, I'm not. Yes, she is. / No, she isn't. Yes, we are / No, we aren't.

Take note!

Spelling: present participle
1 **Normal**   play   + -ing   → play**ing**
2 **Final -e**   write   -e + -ing   → writ**ing**
3 **Short vowel + consonant**
   swi**m** double consonant + -ing → swim**ming**

2 Complete the sentences. Use the present continuous affirmative form of the verbs in the box.

> dance   have   play   wear   win

1 Jack …… the guitar.
2 They …… jeans and trainers.
3 Sandra …… at the party.
4 I …… fun!
5 We …… the football match!

3 Make the sentences in exercise 2 negative.

4 Write questions and affirmative or negative short answers.

> he / dance? (✘)
> *Is he dancing? No, he isn't.*
1 she / swim? (✔)
2 she / have dinner? (✔)
3 he / get dressed? (✘)
4 she / wear a dress? (✘)
5 he / play the violin? (✔)

5 Complete the postcard. Use the present continuous affirmative, negative and interrogative.

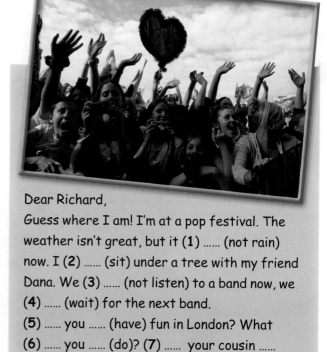

Dear Richard,
Guess where I am! I'm at a pop festival. The weather isn't great, but it (1) …… (not rain) now. I (2) …… (sit) under a tree with my friend Dana. We (3) …… (not listen) to a band now, we (4) …… (wait) for the next band.
(5) …… you …… (have) fun in London? What (6) …… you …… (do)? (7) …… your cousin …… (visit) you? Send me a postcard!
I must go! The band (8) …… (come) now!
Bye. Write soon.
Love Anna

More practice?   **Workbook pages 87–88**

Dialogue

1 🎧 Read and listen. Find Sam in the photo.

DESCRIBING PEOPLE

Emily Do you know Sam?

Joe No, I don't. Is he here?

Emily Yes, over there. He's got short, dark hair and he's wearing jeans and a blue top.

Joe Is he drinking some cola?

Emily That's right.

Joe Is he a friend of yours?

Emily Yes, he is. He sometimes plays volleyball with us. Let's go and talk to him.

2 🎧 Listen and repeat the phrases from the dialogue.

1 He's got short, dark hair.

2 He's wearing jeans.

3 Is he a friend of yours?

3 Practise reading the dialogue.

4 Write your own dialogue. Use the words in the box to help you.

Hair	Clothes	Activities
long / short hair	top	chatting to …
fair / dark hair	jeans	eating a pizza

A: Do you know … ?

B: No, … Is he/she … ?

A: Yes, … He's/She's got … and he's/she's …

B: Is he/she … ?

A: That's …

B: Is he/she a … ?

A: Yes, … He/She sometimes … Let's …

5 Act out your dialogue.

> Do you know … ?

> No, … Is he/she … ?

More practice?	Workbook page 89

Listening

6 🎧 Listen. Which girl is Kirstie? Which girl is Kirstie's sister?

7 🎧 Listen again. Are the sentences true or false? Correct the false sentences.

1 Kirstie is chatting to Martin.

2 Kirstie is wearing jeans and a red jacket.

3 Kirstie and Hannah go to the same school.

4 Kirstie and Hannah are in the same class.

5 Kirstie's sister is drinking orange juice.

GRAMMAR 2

Present continuous with future meaning

> **Take note!**
>
> We can use the present continuous to talk about future plans.
> What are you doing tomorrow?
> I'm playing volleyball.

1 Look at Rob's diary. Write questions and answers about his plans for next weekend.

What's Rob doing on Saturday morning?
He's visiting his grandma.

Saturday	
Morning	visit my grandma
Afternoon	practise the guitar
Evening	go to a pop concert
Sunday	
Morning	play football
Afternoon	watch TV
Evening	meet my friends

Communicate!

Ask your partner four questions about their plans for next weekend.
Are you going shopping?
Yes, I am./No, I'm not

Pronunciation The sounds /ɪ/ and /iː/

2 🎧 Listen. Pay attention to the sounds.

/ɪ/	it	chip
/iː/	eat	cheap

3 🎧 Listen and repeat. Which word do you hear?

1 a) live   b) leave   3 a) its   b) eats
2 a) his   b) he's   4 a) this b) these

should / shouldn't

4 Study the table.

Affirmative	Negative
I should go out	I shouldn't go out
you should go out	you shouldn't go out
he should go out	he shouldn't go out
she should go out	she shouldn't go out
it should go out	it shouldn't go out
we should go out	we shouldn't go out
you should go out	you shouldn't go out
they should go out	they shouldn't go out
	Full form shouldn't = should not

> **Watch out!**
>
> We don't use to after should or shouldn't.
> I should to go home. ✘
> I **should** go home. ✔

5 Read the sentences. Then write advice using should or shouldn't.

There's a bull over there. (go that way)
You shouldn't go that way.

1 This bread is old. (eat it)
2 It's late and I'm tired. (go to bed)
3 She doesn't understand this question. (ask her teacher)
4 This river is dangerous. (go swimming)
5 My uncle doesn't feel very well. (see a doctor)
6 It's our sister's birthday tomorrow. (buy her a present)

Communicate!

Write four more sentences about what you should and shouldn't do in your English classes. Use listen, eat, speak English, drink, and help our friends.
We should listen to our teacher.

| More practice? | Workbook pages 87–88 |

Band fact-file: Green Day

- Green Day are a punk band.
- They are from the USA.
- They started playing together in 1988.
- There are three members, Billie Armstrong, Mike Dirnt and Tré Cool.

This is a photo of Green Day. Billie Armstrong is on the left in the front of the photo. He's singing and jumping. He's wearing different coloured shoes. He was born in 1972 and he's from Rodeo in California.

Tré is in the middle – he's gorgeous!!! He's playing the drums and he's wearing dark clothes. He was born in 1972 and he's from Willits, California.

Mike is on the right. He's playing the bass and he's wearing a black top and black trousers. He was born in 1972, too and he's from Berkeley, California.

Reading

1 Look at the photo. Do you know this group?

2 🎧 Read the text. Copy and complete the fact-file about the band members.

	Billie	Tré	Mike
Instrument			
Clothes			
Age			

Writing Word order

3 Look at the sentences. What is the normal word order in English sentences?
(green = verb, blue = object, red = subject)

He is playing the drums.
Tré is wearing dark clothes.
I am sending a photo.

4 Put the words in the correct order.

1 is playing / Mike / the bass
2 the Internet / surfs / Pam
3 she / is eating / a pizza
4 this / we / don't understand

5 Look at the photo of Linkin Park and the information. Write an email to a friend about them.

	Chester	Brad	Phoenix
Instrument	singer	guitar	bass guitar
Clothes	T-shirt and cap	blue T-shirt	dark blue T-shirt and trousers
Born	1976	1977	1977
Town	Phoenix, Arizona	Glendale, California	Plymouth, Massachusetts

Band fact-file: Linkin Park

Paragraph 1
This is a photo …
Chester is on the left …
He's playing …
He's wearing …
He's was born in … and he's from …

Paragraph 2
Brad is in the middle …

Paragraph 3
Phoenix …

More practice?	Workbook pages 89–90

FOCUS ON THE WORLD

1 🎧 Read the texts. Match them with the photos of the dances.

Music and dance

1 Tango is originally from Argentina but it's becoming popular in other countries too. Men and women dance the tango in pairs. An orchestra usually plays the music. The music is dramatic.

2 Hip-hop is originally from the USA. Men and women dance to hip-hop music, but they don't usually dance in pairs. Men sometimes dance on their heads!

3 Morris dancing is from England. Only men do it. The dancers wear white clothes and the musicians play the accordion.

4 Belly-dancing is originally from India, but it's now very popular in Egypt, Turkey and other countries. Only women do belly-dancing. The music is very fast.

5 Calypso is originally from Trinidad in the West Indies. At carnivals, lots of people dance to calypso music. Bands with metal drums play the music.

A

B

C

D

E

2 🎧 Listen and identify the different kinds of dance music from exercise 1.

3 **MAPS** Find the countries in the texts or mark them on the map on pages 68–9.

4 Which dance music do you like? Work with a partner. Ask and answer.

> Do you like calypso?

> Yes, I do. What about you? Do you like calypso?

> No, I don't.

Song and Reading File page 57

VOCABULARY

Adjectives to describe feelings

1 Complete these sentences about the photo story with adjectives from the box. Look back at the episodes and check, if necessary.

> disappointed embarrassed excited
> surprised nervous

1 Kelly is very ...... when they meet Harry in the chat room and then find out that he is in the same Internet café.
2 Sarah was ...... about going bowling with Harry on her own, so she wanted Kelly to go too.
3 Sarah was ...... because she couldn't go to Harry's party.
4 Kelly was ...... about buying new clothes for the party.
5 Kelly was ...... because she sent the text to Harry by mistake.

Places in town

2 Label the pictures with the words in the box.

> bus stop   cinema   Internet café   library
> post office   school   shopping centre
> supermarket

1 ....

2 ....

3 ....

4 ....

5 ....

6 ....

7 ....

8 ....

Activities

3 Match the verbs (1–8) with the words (a–h).

1 listen   a) the Internet
2 read   b) shopping
3 play   c) computer games
4 surf   d) magazines
5 go   e) volleyball
6 meet   f) to music
7 play   g) to the cinema
8 go   h) friends

Sports

4 Add the sports to the correct group.

> aerobics   basketball   cycling   football
> gymnastics   karate   skiing   surfing   tennis

1 do ......
2 play ......
3 go ......

Instruments and musicians

5 Copy and complete the instuments. Use *a, e, i, o* and *u*.

1 b _ ss   4 g _ _ t _ r   7 s _ x _ ph _ n _
2 c _ ll _   5 k _ yb _ _ rd   8 tr _ mp _ t
3 dr _ ms   6 p _ _ n _   9 v _ _ l _ n

6 Write the musicians who play the instruments in exercise 5.

1 bass guitarist

Clothes

7 Label the clothes.

> trainers   jeans
> jacket   T-shirt
> cap

GRAMMAR

Past simple affirmative (regular)

1 Write the past simple affirmative forms.

1 study   4 arrive
2 stop   5 practise
3 cook   6 chat

2 Complete the sentences. Use the past simple affirmative of the verbs in exercise 1.

1 Kate …… the guitar for three hours last night.
2 My grandad …… French at school.
3 My dad and my sister …… dinner last night.
4 I …… at school at half past eight yesterday morning.
5 It was very quiet when the music ……. .
6 I …… to my friends in the café.

going to

3 Complete the sentences. Use the correct form of *going to*, affirmative or negative.

The weather's terrible. I'm not going to go outside.
1 Gloria can't find her homework. Her teacher …… be pleased.
2 My parents …… go on holiday this year. They haven't got any money.
3 I don't feel very well. I …… go to bed early.
4 Stay for dinner. We …… have pizza and chips.
5 It's raining. You …… get wet.

some and any

4 Write sentences with *there is / are* affirmative, negative and interrogative. Use *some* or *any*.

cheese ✓ milk ✗ pasta ?
There's some cheese. There isn't any milk. Is there any pasta?
1 carrots ✓ bread ✗ biscuits ?
2 rice ✓ apples ✗ lemonade ?
3 soup ✓ chocolate ✗ chicken ?
4 eggs ✓ crisps ✗ sandwiches ?
5 fruit ✓ cake ✗ bananas ?

must / mustn't

5 Rewrite the sentences with *must* or *mustn't*.

Don't run!
You mustn't run.
1 Be careful!
2 Don't worry!
3 Stop!
4 No smoking!
5 Listen to this CD!
6 Don't swim in that river!

Present simple affirmative and negative

6 Complete the sentences. Use the present simple affirmative or negative.

1 We …… (have) lunch at home.
2 They …… (not like) computer games.
3 I …… (not know) the answer.
4 You …… (speak) English very well.
5 He …… (not watch) football on TV.
6 She …… (study) Italian at school.

Present simple interrogative and question words

7 Complete the questions with the words in the box and the present simple interrogative.

How often   What   When   Where
Who   Why

1 …… …… Emily …… (live)? In Manchester.
2 …… …… your dad …… (get up)? At 7.30 a.m.
3 …… …… dolphins …… (eat)? Fish.
4 …… …… you …… (watch) *The Simpsons* every week? Because it's funny.
5 …… …… your sister …… (go) to the cinema with? Her friend Sarah.
6 …… …… …… you …… (play) football? About once a week.

Adverbs of frequency

8 Put the words in the correct order.

1 always / my birthday / forgets / He
2 late / Our teacher / never / is
3 go swimming / often / after school / We
4 sometimes / cheap / are / CDs
5 hungry / I'm / always
6 a football match / We / win / hardly ever

Present continuous

9 Complete the email. Use the present continuous affirmative, negative and interrogative.

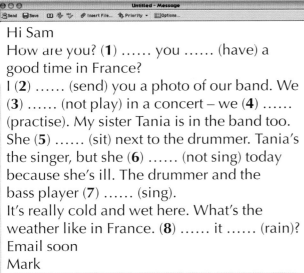

Hi Sam
How are you? (**1**) …… you …… (have) a good time in France?
I (**2**) …… (send) you a photo of our band. We (**3**) …… (not play) in a concert – we (**4**) …… (practise). My sister Tania is in the band too. She (**5**) …… (sit) next to the drummer. Tania's the singer, but she (**6**) …… (not sing) today because she's ill. The drummer and the bass player (**7**) …… (sing).
It's really cold and wet here. What's the weather like in France. (**8**) …… it …… (rain)?
Email soon
Mark

Object pronouns

10 Choose the correct object pronoun.

1 This is my guitar. Do you like **her** / **it**?
2 Christina Aguilera is great. I really like **him** / **her**.
3 English is my favourite subject. I love **him** / **it**.
4 We often phone our cousins, but they never phone **us** / **them**.
5 My friends play football in the park on Saturdays. I sometimes play with **him** / **them**.
6 My aunt lives in Australia. I want to visit **him** / **her**.

Present continuous with future meaning

11 Write questions and true answers.

1 your best friend / do an exam / next week ?
2 your parents / play football / next weekend ?
3 you / cook dinner / this evening ?
4 you / go home /after school ?
5 your friends / visit a museum / this afternoon ?
6 you / go to school / tomorrow ?

should / shouldn't

12 Complete the advice with *should* or *shouldn't*.

1 There are sharks in the sea.
   'You …… swim here.'
2 I'm thirsty.
   'You …… drink some water.'
3 The weather is fantastic today.
   'You …… watch TV all day.'
4 I haven't got any money for the bus.
   'You …… go by bike.'
5 We haven't got any food in the house.
   'You …… go to the supermarket.'

1 Complete the text. Choose the correct words.

1	a) live	b)	lives
2	a) starts	b)	started
3	a) There's	b)	There are
4	a) sing	b)	to sing
5	a) is siting	b)	is sitting
6	a) do	b)	does
7	a) her	b)	him
8	a) some	b)	any
9	a) often listen	b)	listen often
10	a) goes to	b)	is going to
11	a) 'm going to	b)	going to
12	a) should	b)	shouldn't

2 Complete the questions for these answers.

1 .... Patricia study at the School of Performing Arts?
   Music and drama.

2 What ...... she ...... in the photo?
   She's listening to music and singing.

3 ...... is her ...... singer ?
   Robbie Williams.

4 When ...... she ...... move to London.
   Next summer.

5 ...... her teachers always ...... her?
   "You should practise more."

3 Correct the mistakes.

   He **have** got blue eyes. ✗
   He *has* got blue eyes. ✔

1 We **study** Italian last year. ✗
2 There isn't **some** bread. ✗
3 We **no study** French. ✗
4 **Want you** to watch TV? ✗
5 **How** is your name? ✗
6 **He wearing** a jacket? ✗
7 **It not** raining at the moment. ✗
8 **Do you can** swim? ✗
9 Tomorrow evening I **play** football. ✗
10 You **shouldn't to shout** in class. ✗

This is Patricia. She's 14 and she **(1)** ...... in Liverpool. She **(2)** ...... last month at the School of Performing Arts, studying music and drama. **(3)** ...... 150 students at the school. She plays the piano and guitar, and she can **(4)** ...... too. In the photo, she **(5)** ...... in her bedroom, listening to music. Her favourite singer is Robbie Williams. Why **(6)** ...... she like **(7)** ...... ? 'Because there are **(8)** ...... great songs on his CDs. I **(9)** ...... to them in my bedroom.'
After her exams next summer she **(10)** ...... move to London. She wants to sing in pop videos. 'I **(11)** ...... be a singer, I know it', says Patricia. 'But my teachers always tell me I **(12)** ...... practise more.'

4 Television

WHAT'S IN THIS UNIT?

- Television programmes
- Adjectives
- Comparative adjectives
- Superlative adjectives
- Giving opinions
- *because*

VOCABULARY

Television programmes

1 🎧 Listen and repeat.

1 cartoon

2 soap opera

3 documentary

4 quiz show

5 chat show

6 sports programme

7 comedy

8 police drama

9 reality TV programme

10 the news

2 🎧 Listen and identify the types of TV programme.

3 Think of examples of the TV programmes in exercise 1.

   1 *The Simpsons is a cartoon.*

4 In pairs, ask and answer.

> Do you like quiz shows?

> Yes, I do. / No, I don't.

More practice?   **Workbook page 91**

SARAH'S STORY

Big sister

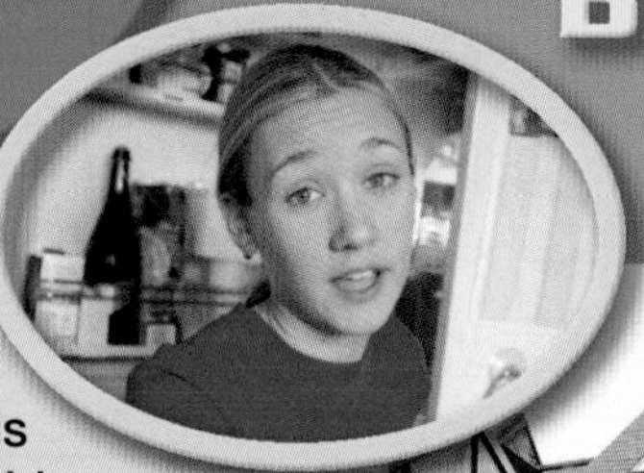

1 During the week, I often look after my younger brother Luke in the evenings because my mum works. But at the weekend, I go out with my friends. Today is Saturday, and Kelly and I are at one of the biggest and most famous markets in London: Portobello Road. We're talking about TV programmes.

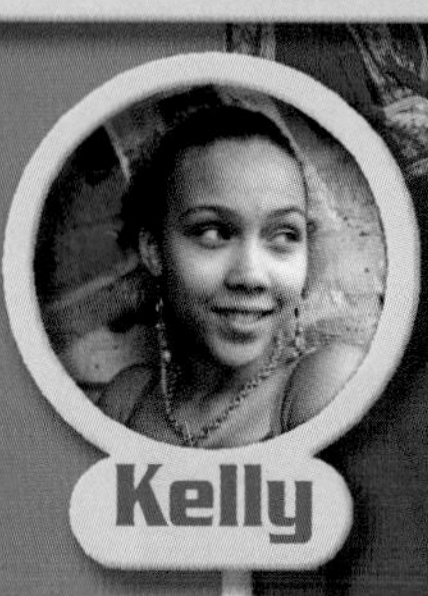

Kelly

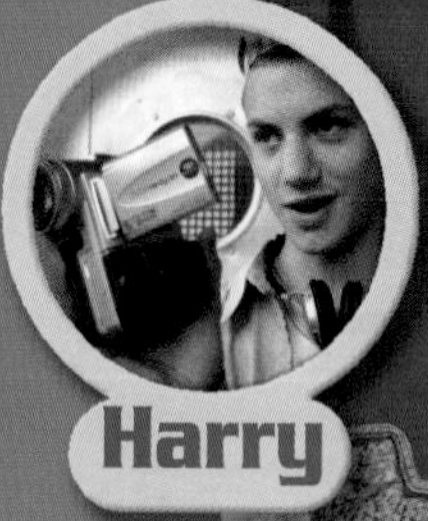

Harry

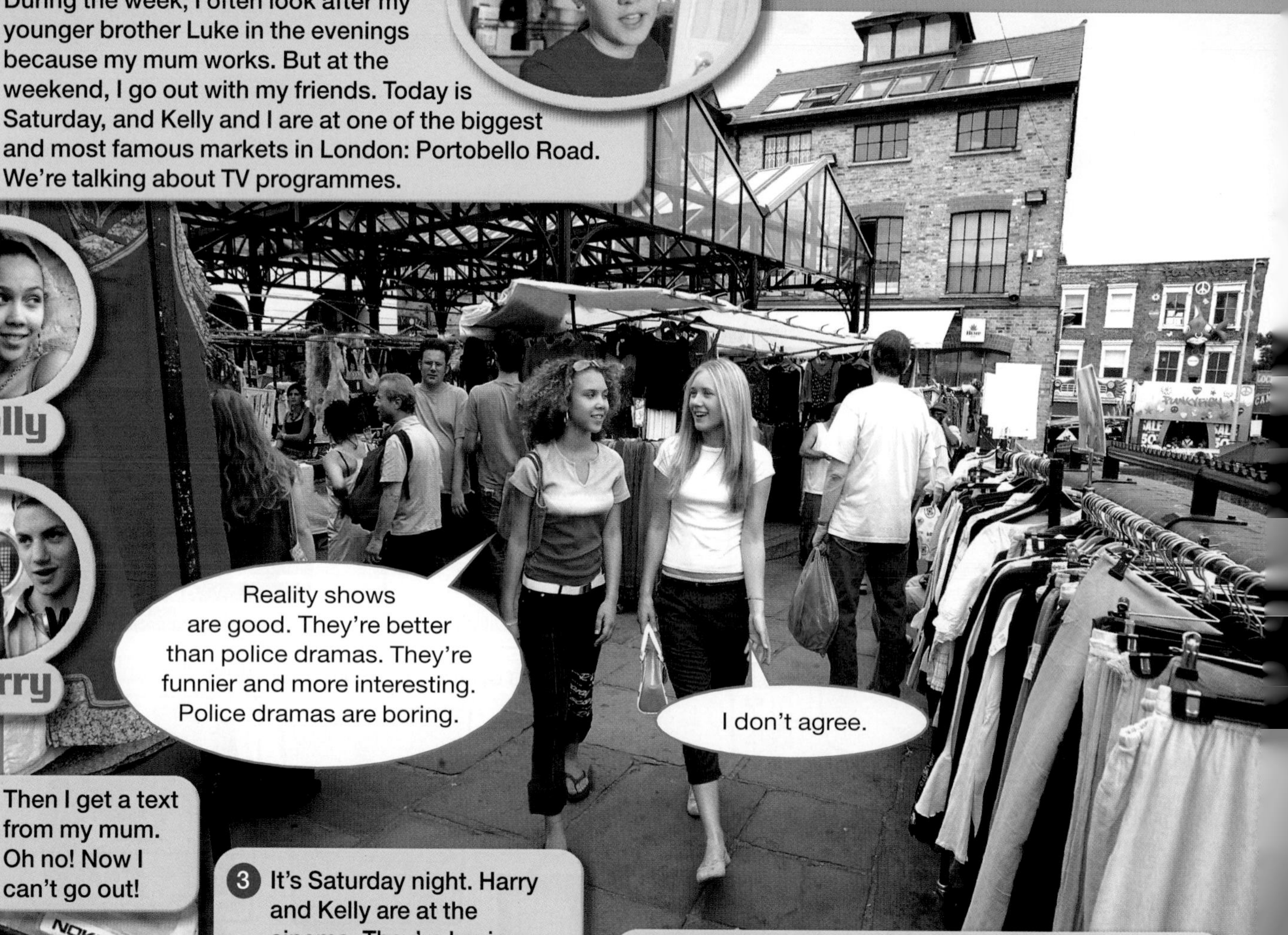

> Reality shows are good. They're better than police dramas. They're funnier and more interesting. Police dramas are boring.

> I don't agree.

2 Then I get a text from my mum. Oh no! Now I can't go out!

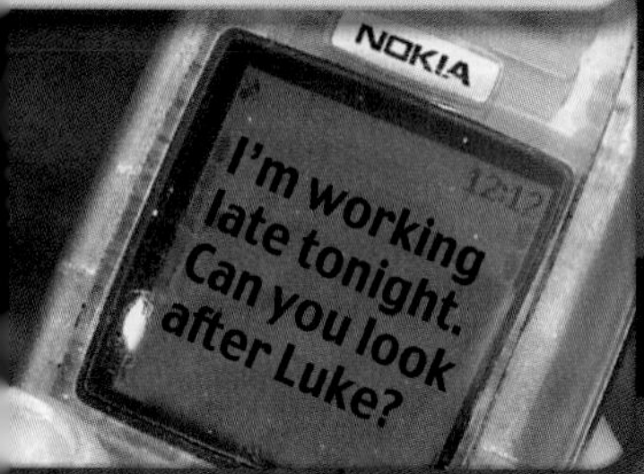

> I'm working late tonight. Can you look after Luke?

3 It's Saturday night. Harry and Kelly are at the cinema. They're having a better evening than I am! I'm at home with Luke. I want to watch Law and Order, my favourite police drama, but I'm still cleaning the kitchen. And Luke is always more difficult when Mum isn't here …

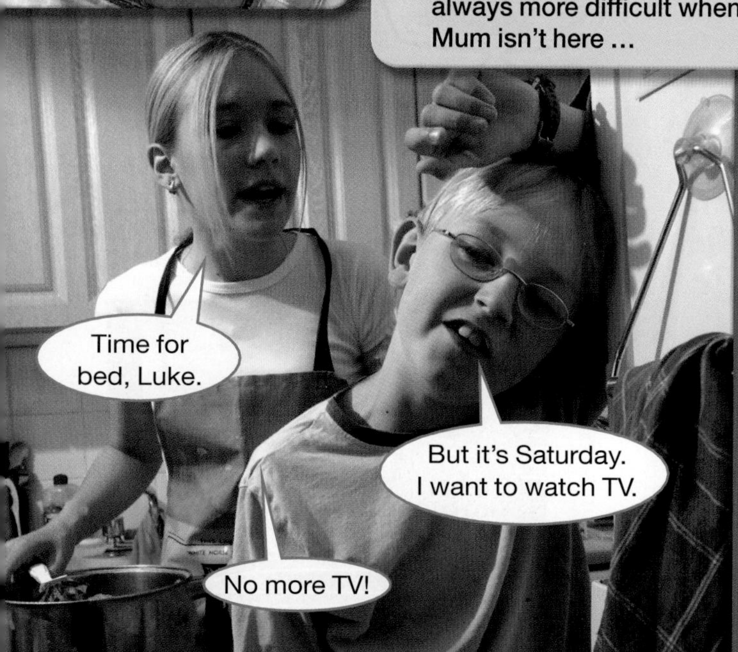

4 Finally, Luke is in bed. The house is a lot quieter! Now I can watch Law and Order! Then I get a text from Kelly.

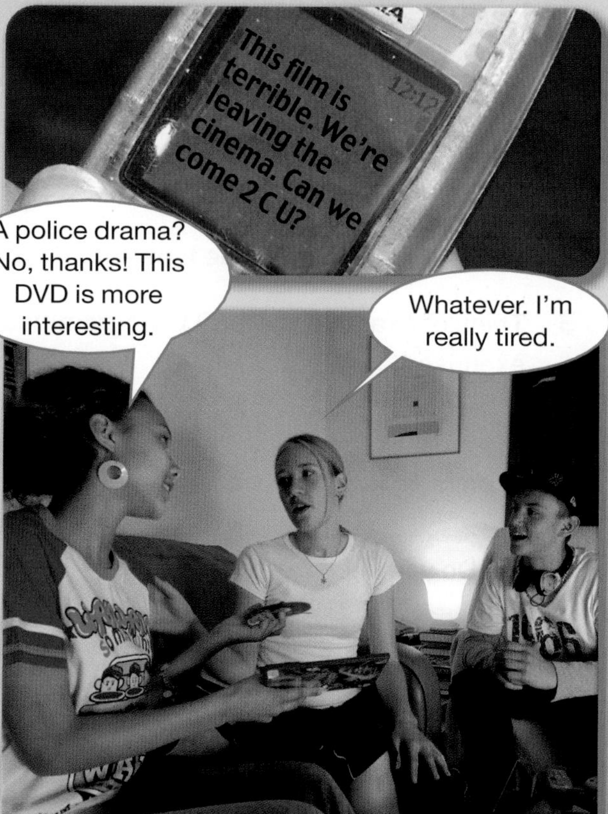

> This film is terrible. We're leaving the cinema. Can we come 2 C U?

> A police drama? No, thanks! This DVD is more interesting.

> Whatever. I'm really tired.

> Time for bed, Luke.

> But it's Saturday. I want to watch TV.

> No more TV!

1 🎧 Read and listen. What does Sarah want to watch on TV?

2 Correct the sentences.

1 Kelly and Sarah are at a **sports centre**.
2 Kelly and Sarah are talking about **films**.
3 Kelly **likes** police dramas.
4 Sarah's mum has to **go shopping** in the evening.
5 Luke wants to **play computer games**.
6 Kelly wants to **listen to a CD**.

3 **REAL ENGLISH** Who says these expressions? What do they mean?

> 1 I don't agree.

> 2 Time for bed.

> 3 No, thanks!

> 4 Whatever.

Teen focus

Helping out at home
Read what Sarah says about life at home. Do you look after younger brothers or sisters, or help with the housework?

> My mum and dad are divorced, so my mum has to work and look after me and Luke. I try to help her. I do some housework and I sometimes look after my little brother.

Word check   Adjectives

4 Find the opposites of these adjectives in the story.

bad	**(1)** ……
interesting	**(2)** ……
fantastic	**(3)** ……

Watch out!

Adjectives go before nouns in English.
~~A documentary interesting~~ ✗
An interesting documentary ✔

5 Match the opposites (1–8) with (a–h).

   1 young – e old

1 young   a) cold
2 short   b) happy
3 hot   c) difficult
4 sad   d) new
5 old   e) old
6 easy   f) tall
7 long   g) short
8 small   h) large

Study skills

Analyzing your mistakes

6 Look at the underlined mistakes. What kinds of mistake are they? Match them with these labels (a–d).

a spelling
b vocabulary
c grammar
d word order

1 My dad is <u>more taller</u> than my mum.
2 My brother is a <u>mecanic</u>.
3 Friends is <u>a programme funny</u>.
4 My sister has got <u>large</u>, dark hair.

7 Now correct the mistakes.

More practice?	Workbook page 91

GRAMMAR 1

Comparative adjectives

1 Study the table.

Short adjectives		
Adjective	Rule	Comparative
old	+ -er	older
large	+ -r	larger
hot	double consonant + -er	hotter
funny	-y → -ier	funnier
good	irregular	better
bad		worse

2 Write the comparative forms of these adjectives.

1 rich   3 good   5 bad
2 wide   4 big   6 easy

> **Take note!**
>
> We use *than* to make comparisons.
> Lisa is shorter **than** Chris.

3 Complete the sentences. Use the comparative form of the short adjectives.

1 Tiny is ...... than Sky. (tall)
2 Sky is ...... at basketball than Tiny. (good)
3 Tiny is ...... than Sky. (fast)
4 Sky's shorts are ...... than Tiny's shorts. (wide)
5 Tiny's hair is ...... than Sky's hair. (long)
6 Sky's feet are ...... than Tiny's feet. (big)

4 Study the table.

Long adjectives		
Adjective	Rule	Comparative
expensive	more + adjective	more expensive
boring		more boring

5 Complete the sentences. Use the comparative form of the long adjectives. Which sentences do you agree with?

1 Penélope Cruz is ...... than Julia Roberts. (beautiful)
2 History is ...... than English. (difficult)
3 Friends are ...... than money. (important)
4 Documentaries are ...... than police dramas. (interesting)
5 Basketball is ...... than football. (popular)
6 Dogs are ...... than cats. (intelligent)

Communicate!

> Write five sentences about people in your class. Use comparatives. Compare with a partner.
> Carolina is taller than Ana.

More practice?   Workbook pages 92–93

Pronunciation The weak vowel /ə/

6 🎧 Listen and repeat. Pay attention to the weak vowel /ə/.

1 This film is better than that film.
2 *Malcolm* is funnier than *Buffy*.
3 June is hotter than March.
4 Your hair is longer than my hair.

Dialogue

1 🎧 **Read and listen. Complete the dialogue with the words in the box.**

> cartoons   favourite   funnier   great   prefer

GIVING OPINIONS

Joe What's your (**1**) ...... TV programme?
Emily *Friends*. I think it's (**2**) ...... !
Joe So do I. But I (**3**) ...... *The Simpsons*.
Emily Really? Why?
Joe In my opinion, *The Simpsons* is (**4**) ...... than *Friends*.
Emily I don't agree. I don't think (**5**) ...... are very funny.

2 🎧 **Listen and repeat the phrases from the dialogue.**

1	I think it's great!	**4**	In my opinion, …
2	So do I.	**5**	I don't agree.
3	I prefer *The Simpsons*.		

3 **Practise reading the dialogue.**

4 **Write your own dialogue. Use the adjectives in the box to help you.**

> interesting   funny   exciting   good / better

A: What's …
B: … I think …
A: So … But I …
B: Really? … ?
A: In my …
B: I don't … I don't think …

5 **Act out your dialogue.**

What's … ?

… I think …

More practice?	Workbook page 94

Listening

6 🎧 **Listen to Alex and Hannah. Answer the questions.**

1 What's Hannah's favourite sport?
2 What's Alex's favourite sport?
3 Who's Hannah's favourite pop star?
4 Who's Alex's favourite pop star?

7 🎧 **Listen again. Complete the sentences. Use the words in the box.**

> more beautiful   more exciting   prefer
> the best   the most exciting

1 I ...... football.
2 Football is ...... than volleyball.
3 Volleyball is ...... sport in the world.
4 Dido is ...... singer in the world.
5 Anastacia is ...... than Dido.

GRAMMAR 2

Superlative adjectives

1 Study the table.

Short adjectives		
Adjective	Rule	Superlative
old	+ -est	the oldest
large	+ -st	the largest
hot	double consonant + -est	the hottest
funny	-y → -iest	the funniest
good	irregular	the best
bad		the worst

2 Complete the sentences. Use the superlative form of the short adjectives.

1 This is ...... (wet) day of the week.
2 Juan is ...... (tall) boy in the class.
3 Our classroom has got ...... (large) blackboard in the school.
4 Which is ...... (easy) – English, PE or maths?
5 June 21st is ...... (long) day of the year.
6 Is cola ...... (good) drink in the world?

3 Complete the sentences. Use a word from the box and the superlative form of the short adjectives.

> Amazon Antarctica ~~Atacama~~ Jupiter
> McCartney Pan-American Tiger

The Atacama Desert is the driest place in the world. (dry)

1 ...... is ...... planet in the Solar System. (big)
2 The ...... is ...... river in the world. (wide)
3 ...... Woods is ...... golfer in the world. (good)
4 Paul ...... is ...... pop star in the UK. (rich)
5 The ...... Highway is ...... road in the world. (long)
6 ...... is ...... place in the world. (windy)

4 Study the table.

Long adjectives		
Adjective	Rule	Superlative
expensive	the most + adjective	the most expensive
popular		the most popular

5 Write sentences with the superlative form of the long adjectives.

Law and Order / popular / police drama / in the USA.
Law and Order is the most popular police drama in the USA.

1 Tokyo / expensive / city / in the world
2 Chinese / difficult / language / in the world
3 The hippo / dangerous / animal / in Africa
4 Beckham / famous / footballer / in the world
5 Dublin / exciting / city / in Ireland

6 What do you think? Complete the questions with *What's* or *Who's*. Then ask and answer in pairs.

What's the most exciting programme on TV?
I think it's *Angel*.

1 ...... the best cartoon on TV?
2 ...... the most beautiful film star in the world?
3 ...... the worst programme on TV?
4 ...... the funniest comedy on TV?
5 ...... the best actor in the world?

More practice? Workbook pages 92–93

My favourite TV programme

by Isabel

I think *Malcolm in the Middle* is the best programme on TV. It's an American comedy about a boy, his family and his friends. I usually watch it with my friends because we all like it.

The most important characters are Malcolm and his three brothers, Reese, Francis and Dewey. Reese is older than Malcolm. They argue a lot. The oldest brother is Francis and Dewey is the youngest. Malcolm goes to a special school because he's very intelligent. His school friends are very intelligent too – but they're strange!

I like *Malcolm in the Middle* because it's really funny. The actors are fantastic and there's often good music in the programme too.

Reading

1 🎧 Look at the photo of *Malcolm in the Middle*. Which sentence do you agree with?

   a) In my opinion, *Malcolm in the Middle* is really funny.
   b) I don't like *Malcolm in the Middle*.
   c) I don't know this TV programme.

2 Read the text. Answer the questions.

   1 Who does Isabel usually watch *Malcolm in the Middle* with?
   2 How many brothers has Malcolm got?
   3 Which brother is the oldest?
   4 Which brother is the youngest?
   5 Why does Malcolm go to a special school?
   6 Why does Isabel like the programme?

Writing *because*

3 Study the information.

> **Take note!**
>
> We use *because* to join ideas together and give a reason.
> I like *Malcolm in the Middle*. It's really funny.
> I like *Malcolm in the Middle* **because** it's really funny.

4 Match sentences (1–6) with sentences (a–f). Write the sentences and join them together with *because*.

   1-d I love soap operas because they're really interesting.

   1 I love soap operas.   a) It's cold today.
   2 I hate quiz shows.   b) You're very funny.
   3 I'm wearing a jacket.   c) I'm good at it.
   4 I'm wearing shorts.   d) They're really interesting.
   5 I like you.   e) It's hot and sunny.
   6 I like maths.   f) They're really boring.

5 Write about your favourite TV programme. Use the writing plan to help you.

> **Paragraph 1: Introduction**
> I think ... is the best programme on TV.
> It's a ... about ...
> I watch it with ...
> **Paragraph 2: Characters**
> The most important characters are ...
> (What are they like? What do they do?)
> **Paragraph 3: My opinion**
> I like ... because ...

More practice?   Workbook pages 94–95

FOCUS ON THE WORLD

1 Look at the photos. Can you name the director or any of the actors?

2 🎧 Read the information.

CINEMA

The richest

1 American film stars are very famous and very rich. Julia Roberts gets about $20 million for every film and Tom Hanks gets about $25 million. The richest film director is probably George Lucas, the director of the Star Wars films. He gets about $200 million a year.

The biggest

2 Hollywood is the name of the famous film industry in the USA. It makes about 600 films a year, but it isn't the biggest film industry in the world. 'Bollywood', the film industry in Mumbai, India, is bigger than Hollywood. It makes about 1,000 films a year. Every day, 15 million people watch Bollywood films!

The most successful

3 Big box office films from 2003 to 2005 were:
1 *The Lord of the Rings: The Return Of The King* (2003)
2 *Spider-Man 2* (2004)
3 *Shrek 2* (2004)
4 *Harry Potter and the Prisoner Of Azkaban* (2004)
5 *Star Wars III – Revenge Of The Sith* (2005)

---

3 Answer the questions.

1 How much does Tom Hanks get for every film?
2 How many films does Hollywood make every year?
3 What is 'Bollywood'?
4 How many people watch Bollywood films every day?
5 How many of the five big box office films do you know?

4 MAPS Find or mark Hollywood and Mumbai on the map on pages 68–9.

5 In pairs, ask and answer.

1 How often do you go to the cinema?
2 Do you like American films?
3 What's your favourite film?
4 Who are your favourite film stars?

Song and Reading File page 57.

5 People in the past

WHAT'S IN THIS UNIT?

- Jobs
- Places of work
- Past simple affirmative (negative and interrogative irrregular verbs)
- Past simple affirmative (regular and irregular verbs)
- could / couldn't
- Talking about your weekend
- Using notes

VOCABULARY

Jobs

1 🎧 Listen and repeat.

1 bus driver
2 mechanic
3 writer
4 shop assistant
5 secretary
6 actor
7 politician
8 artist
9 police officer
10 hairdresser
11 composer
12 nurse

2 🎧 Listen and identify the jobs.

3 What were these people's jobs?

1 Jorge Luis Borges
2 Frida Kahlo
3 Simón Bolívar
4 Astor Piazzolla

| **More practice?** | **Workbook page 96** |

1 Last week, we had to do a project for school about a famous person from the past. But who? We thought about famous writers, artists and politicians, but we couldn't decide. We only had one more day to do the project. In the end, we went to a shop in town and looked at the magazines. We were lucky. We found the perfect person!

Kelly

Sarah

What about Elvis? He died in 1977.

Great idea. I love Elvis.

2 We didn't have time to write the project, so we made a documentary film instead. Sarah knew a lot about Elvis. For example, Elvis sold more than a billion records worldwide and he made 31 films as an actor. Kelly didn't know much about Elvis, but she's good at talking! I didn't appear in the film. I was the director – and the cameraman.

3 I edited the film on computer at home. Then, I copied the film onto a disk and gave it to Mr Thomas, our teacher. He didn't watch it immediately – he took it away with him. The next day, Kelly and Sarah came round to my house …

This is Sarah. She became an Elvis fan before she could talk.

That's right! And when I was four, my dad took me to the theatre to see a play about Elvis.

Are you ready?

I gave our film to Mr Thomas.

You're a hero!

So what's this? Another copy?

4 It was too late. I gave our teacher the wrong disk! He didn't have our film. He had a film of my sister washing her dog!

1 🎧 **Read and listen. Put the events in order.**

1 Sarah, Kelly and Harry made a film.
2 Harry gave a disk to Mr Thomas.
3 Sarah, Kelly and Harry read some magazines.

2 Correct the sentences.

1 The friends made a **comedy** film for their school project.
2 The film was about **Princess Diana**.
3 **Kelly** knew a lot about Elvis.
4 Elvis made 31 films as a **director**.
5 Sarah saw a **film** about Elvis when she was four.
6 **Kelly** gave Mr Thomas a disk.

3 REAL ENGLISH Who says these expressions? What do they mean?

1 We were lucky.

2 Are you ready?

3 So what's this?

4 It was too late.

Teen focus

Music from the past
Read what Harry says about music from the past. What's your opinion?

Most of my friends only know music that's in the charts now. That's a shame, because there's lots of good pop music from the past: Elvis, The Beatles, The Rolling Stones. They were all great musicians. I often listen to my parents', and my grandparents', CDs'.

Word check Places of work

4 In the story, find the places where these people work.

1 actor
2 shop assistant

5 Match the jobs (1–5) with the places of work (a–e).

1	secretary	a)	police station
2	mechanic	b)	hospital
3	police officer	c)	office
4	nurse	d)	hair salon
5	hairdresser	e)	garage

Study skills

Revising grammar

6 Here are some ways you can use *Flashlight* when you revise grammar.

- Look at the tables and explanations on the grammar pages in the unit.
- Look at the story pages and find examples of the grammar.
- Check that you can do the practice exercises on the grammar pages in the unit.
- Use the Workbook pages for extra practice.
- Check that you can do the practice exercises in the Revision units.

7 On which pages of this book can you find these grammar points? Remember to look in the main units and the revision units.

1 *must / mustn't*
2 Present continuous
3 Comparative adjectives
4 Adverbs of frequency
5 *going to*

| More practice? | Workbook page 96 |

GRAMMAR 1

Past simple affirmative (irregular verbs)

1 🎧 Match the base forms (1–10) with the past simple forms (a–j). Then listen and check your answers.

1	be	**a)**	went
2	become	**b)**	found
3	find	**c)**	wrote
4	go	**d)**	was/were
5	have	**e)**	made
6	leave	**f)**	had
7	make	**g)**	became
8	meet	**h)**	met
9	win	**i)**	left
10	write	**j)**	won

> **Take note!**
>
> *was* and *were* are the past simple forms of *be*. We use *was* with *I*, *he*, *she* and *it*. We use *were* with *you*, *we* and *they*.
>
> Marilyn Monroe **was** an actress.
> Kahlo and Solar **were** artists.

2 Complete the sentences. Use the past simple form of the irregular verbs from exercise 1.

1 Elvis Presley …… 31 films.
2 The actor Viggo Mortensen …… to New York in 1969.
3 The writer Borges …… *The Aleph*.
4 The singer Carlos Gardel …… Argentinian.
5 The composer Bach …… twenty children.
6 The writer Pablo Neruda …… the Nobel Prize for Literature in 1971.

3 Write sentences. Change the present simple to the past simple.

1 He leaves school at four o'clock.
2 I write the answers in my notebook.
3 We meet our friends at the café.
4 They chat to their teacher after the lesson.
5 He worries a lot about his exams.
6 I phone my grandad every day.

4 Complete the text. Use the past simple form of the regular and irregular verbs in the box.

be	become	die	find	leave	live
make	move	visit			

Charlie Chaplin, the famous actor and film director, was born in London in 1889. His parents (**1**) …… singers.
  Chaplin (**2**) …… school when he was only ten years old and (**3**) …… an actor.
  Chaplin (**4**) …… the USA in 1913 and (**5**) …… a job at a film studio. In 1914 he (**6**) …… 35 films!
  He (**7**) …… there until 1952, then he (**8**) …… to Switzerland. He (**9**) …… in Vevey in 1977 at the age of 88.

Communicate!

Write three sentences about a famous person.
He/She was a … (job)
He/She was born in … (year)
He/She lived in … (city/country)
Tell your partner about them.

More practice?   **Workbook pages 97–98**

Dialogue

1 🎧 **Read and listen. Complete the dialogue with the words in the box.**

> about   couldn't   happened   interesting
> weekend

TALKING ABOUT YOUR WEEKEND

Joe	How was your (**1**) ...... ?
Alex	It was great. We went to the National Football Museum.
Joe	Was it (**2**) ...... ?
Emily	Yes, we had a great time. We saw an exhibition about women's football.
Joe	Really?
Emily	What (**3**) ...... you? How was your weekend?
Joe	It was terrible.
Alex	Why? What (**4**) ...... ?
Joe	We had tickets for a football match, but I was ill, so we (**5**) ...... go.

2 🎧 **Listen and repeat the phrases from the dialogue.**

1 How was your weekend?
2 We had a great time.
3 What about you?

3 **Practise reading the dialogue.**

4 **Write your own dialogue. Use the ideas in the box to help you or use your own ideas.**

Ideas for A
MALBA in Buenos Aires – saw some paintings by Solar
Quinta Vergara Park in Viña del Mar, – saw the beautiful gardens

Ideas for B
tickets for the cinema
tickets for the theatre

A: How was ... ?
B: It was ... We went ...
A: Was ... ?
B: Yes, we ... We saw ...
A: Really?
B: What about ... ? How ... ?
A: It was ...
B: Why? What ... ?
A: We had tickets ... but ...

5 **Act out your dialogue.**

> How was ... ?

> It was ... We went ...

More practice?	Workbook page 99

Listening

6 🎧 **Listen. Choose the correct names.**

1 **Hannah** / **Alex** went to the cinema.
2 **Hannah** / **Alex** went to London.

7 🎧 **Listen again. Answer the questions.**

1 Was the film good?
2 Where did Hannah go on Sunday?
3 Why did they come home early?
4 What did Alex and his family do in Oxford Street?
5 What did Alex buy?
6 Why wasn't Alex's dad very happy?

GRAMMAR 2

Past simple negative and interrogative

1 Study the table.

Negative	Interrogative
I didn't go	Did I go …?
you didn't go	Did you go …?
he didn't go	Did he go …?
she didn't go	Did she go …?
it didn't go	Did it go …?
we didn't go	Did we go …?
you didn't go	Did you go …?
they didn't go	Did they go …?
Full forms	**Short answers**
didn't = did not	Yes, I did. / No, I didn't.
	Yes, she did. / No, she didn't.

Watch out!

We use the base form in negative and interrogative sentences.

Pele didn't played football for Argentina. ✘
Pele didn't play football for Argentina. ✔
Did Mozart lived in Salzburg? ✘
Did Mozart live in Salzburg? ✔

2 Write negative, affirmative and interrogative sentences.

John Lennon died in 1990. (1980)
John Lennon didn't die in 1990.
When did John Lennon die?
He died in 1980.

1 Elvis Presley lived in Britain. (the USA)
2 Jorge Luis Borges wrote music. (books)
3 Marilyn Monroe died in 1952. (1962)
4 Raimundo Orsi played football for Brazil. (Argentina)
5 Stan Laurel met Oliver Hardy in New York. (Hollywood)

Pronunciation   The sound /h/

3   🎧 Listen and repeat. Which word do you hear?

1 **a)** at   **b)** hat   3 **a)** air   **b)** hair
2 **a)** old   **b)** hold   4 **a)** it   **b)** hit

could / couldn't

4 Study the table. Are the *he/she/it* forms different?

Affirmative	Negative
I could swim	I couldn't swim
you could swim	you couldn't swim
he could swim	he couldn't swim
she could swim	she couldn't swim
it could swim	it couldn't swim
we could swim	we couldn't swim
you could swim	you couldn't swim
they could swim	they couldn't swim
could is the past of *can*.	**Full form** couldn't = could not

5 Write sentences about the famous people. Use *could* or *couldn't*.

Albert Einstein / not read / eight
Albert Einstein couldn't read when he was eight.

1 Mozart / play the piano / three
2 Picasso / draw / two
3 Venus Williams / play tennis / four
4 Ian Thorpe / not swim / seven
5 Gary Kasparov / play chess / five

6 Now write questions for your partner.

read / three?
Could you read when you were three?

1 swim / eight?
2 count to 100 / five?
3 write your name / six?
4 talk / one?
5 walk / two?

7 Ask and answer the questions in exercise 6.

Could you read when you were three?

Yes, I could. / No, I couldn't.

More practice?   Workbook pages 97-98

William Shakespeare

William Shakespeare was born in Stratford-upon-Avon in England in 1564. Shakespeare was an actor and a writer. He wrote thirty-seven plays. Shakespeare started school in Stratford when he was seven years old. He studied Latin. The school day was very long. In the summer, lessons started at six o'clock in the morning and finished at five o'clock in the afternoon. Shakespeare left school when he was about thirteen.

In 1582 he moved to London. First, he worked as an actor. Then, he started to write plays. He became very rich and successful. He died in Stratford on 23rd April 1616, his birthday. On exactly the same day, another great writer died in Madrid. His name was Miguel de Cervantes.

Reading

1 🎧 Read the text. Then copy and complete the notes about Shakespeare.

Born (where and when?)	Born in … in …
Jobs	Actor and …
Plays	Wrote … plays
School	Started in … when he was … Left school when he was …
Career	In … moved to … Worked as … Started to write … Became … and …
Died (where and when?)	Died in … on …

Writing Using notes

2 Write full sentences about Salvador Dalí from these notes.

Dalí – born in Figueras, 1904
Dalí was born in Figueras in 1904.

1 started at art school, Madrid, 1921
2 visited Paris, 1928, met Picasso
3 moved to the USA, 1940
4 returned to Spain, 1948
5 died in Figueras, 1989

3 Write a text about Frida Kahlo. Use the notes below and the text in exercise 1 to help you.

Born	6th July 1907 Mexico City
Job	painter
School	National Preparatory School
Career	1925, seriously injured in bus accident. Started painting. 1929, married Diego Rivera. 1953, first and only exhibition in Mexico.
Died	13th July 1954, Mexico City.

| More practice? | Workbook pages 99–100 |

FOCUS ON THE WORLD

1 🎧 Read the text.

Madame Tussaud

Madame Tussaud was born in France in 1761. She wasn't from a rich family, but she became a successful businesswoman. She made wax models of politicians and other important people. In 1802, she came to the UK with an exhibition of her wax models.

In 1835, Madame Tussaud opened a permanent exhibition in London. She died in 1850, but her exhibition is still very popular. Two and a half million people visit it every year. There are Madame Tussaud exhibitions in other cities too – Las Vegas, New York, Amsterdam and Hong Kong.

The exhibitions have wax models of famous people from the present and the past. There are actors, politicians, kings, queens and pop stars.

2 Are these sentences true or false? Correct the false sentences.

1 Madame Tussaud was born in 1761.
2 She was from a rich family.
3 She came to the UK in 1820.
4 She opened an exhibition in London in 1835.
5 She was 70 years old when she died.
6 There are Madame Tussaud exhibitions in the USA.

3 Look at the photos of wax models from the Madame Tussaud exhibition in London. Can you name them?

4 MAPS Find or mark Las Vegas, New York, Amsterdam and Hong Kong on the map on pages 68–9.

Song and Reading File page 57.

VOCABULARY

Television programmes

1 Match the TV programmes to the pictures.

> cartoon   chat show   comedy
> police drama   quiz show
> sports programme   soap opera   the news

1

2

3

4

5

6

7

8

Adjectives

2 Find 14 adjectives.

sadtallyoungoldcoldboringlongeasyhotinterestingshortdifficulthappynew

3 Put the adjectives from exercise 2 in pairs of opposites. Which adjectives have *two* opposites?

Jobs and places of work

4 Read the sentences and complete the puzzle. What's the secret word?

1 A ...... works in a garage.
2 A ...... works in a shop.
3 Tony Blair is a ....
4 An ...... works in a theatre.
5 A ...... drives buses.
6 Kahlo was an ....
7 A ...... works in a police station.
8 Piazzolla was a ....
9 A ...... works in a hospital.
10 Borges was a ....
11 A ...... works in an office.

1		M	E	C	H	A	N	I	C		
2	S		P			S		T			T
3		P					C		N		
4	A										
5		B					V		R		
6			A					T			
7	P	L			O			C		R	
8	C	M				R					
9		N			E						
10	W	R			R						
11		S				T			Y		

GRAMMAR

Superlative adjectives

1 Complete the sentences. Use the superlative forms of the short adjectives.

1 The Nile is ...... (long) river in the world.
2 The Pacific is ...... (wide) ocean in the world.
3 Andagoya in Colombia is ...... (wet) city in the world.
4 The Giant Redwood is ...... (tall) tree in the world.
5 *The Simpsons* is ...... (funny) programme on TV.

2 Write sentences about the computer games. Use the superlative form of the long adjectives in the chart.

1 'Army Combat' is the most expensive game.

		Alien Invasion	Army Combat	Planet Wars
1	expensive	€20	€25	€15
2	exciting	★★	★	★★★
3	difficult	★★★	★★	★
4	popular	★	★★★	★★
5	modern	★★★	★	★★

Comparative adjectives

3 Complete the sentences. Use the comparative forms of the short adjectives.

1 The Nile is (long) than the Amazon.
2 Trains are (fast) than cars.
3 Africa is (hot) than Europe.
4 Mark is (good) at maths than Helen.
5 Ben is (funny) than Liam.

4 Complete the sentences. Use the comparative forms of the long adjectives.

1 Chat shows are interesting but reality TV programmes are ....
2 Crocodiles are dangerous but tigers are ....
3 *Malcolm in the Middle* is popular but *The Simpsons* is ....
4 John is intelligent but Ellen is ....
5 Science is difficult but maths is ....
6 Silver is expensive but gold is ....
7 Sharon Stone is beautiful but Halle Berry is ....

Past simple affirmative (irregular)

5 Complete the sentences. Use the past simple affirmative of the verbs in brackets.

Astor Piazolla *was* (be) a composer.
1 I ...... (find) some money under the sofa in the living room.
2 I ...... (leave) home early yesterday morning.
3 She ...... (write) a letter to her aunt in the USA.
4 We ...... (go) to Scotland by plane.
5 James Dean and River Phoenix ...... (be) actors.
6 They ...... (meet) their friends at the cinema.

Past simple negative

6 Make these sentences negative.

1 We caught the train to Liverpool.
2 They arrived late.
3 She left home at eight o'clock.
4 You came to my party.
5 He played computer games last night.
6 I had pasta for dinner last night.
7 I met my friends at the disco.
8 We won the football match.

Past simple interrogative

7 Look at the chart. Write questions and short answers about Marta. Use the past simple.

Did Marta surf the Internet yesterday? Yes, she did.

Yesterday ...

1 surf the Internet	✔
2 have a shower	✔
3 play basketball	✘
4 listen to music	✘
5 go to the cinema	✘
6 meet her friends	✔
7 write a letter	✔

could / couldn't

8 Write sentences about Charlie. Use *could* or *couldn't* and the verbs in the box.

count to ten   draw   play football   ~~swim~~
walk   write his name

Charlie / three
Charlie couldn't swim when he was three.

1 Charlie / one
2 Charlie and his friend / four
3 Charlie / three
4 Charlie / two
5 Charlie / three

1 Complete Patricia's letter. Choose the correct words.

1	a) I send	b)	I'm sending
2	a) couldn't	b)	not could
3	a) haven't got	b)	don't have got
4	a) have	b)	has
5	a) the most good	b)	the best
6	a) easier	b)	more easy
7	a) went	b)	goed
8	a) meet	b)	met
9	a) 's going to	b)	'm going to
10	a) went out	b)	go out
11	a) saw	b)	see
12	a) not played	b)	didn't play

2 Match the names (1–6) with the phrases (a–f). Write sentences.

1	Patricia	a)	danced with Patricia.
2	Karen	b)	is writing the letter in Karen's room.
3	Patricia and Karen	c)	was on TV last night.
4	A really nice boy	d)	are having guitar lessions together.
5	Robbie Williams	e)	is the best guitarist in the school.

3 Correct the mistakes.

The train **leave** at 5:35. ✗
The train leaves at 5:35.

1 My brother is **swiming** in the sea. ✗
2 History is **more interesting that** maths. ✗
3 We **watchd** TV last night. ✗
4 I **studyd** Italian at school last year. ✗
5 Susan and I **chated** about school. ✗
6 **Did you was** at Dave's party? ✗
7 Who **winned** the football match? ✗
8 I **no could** find my Shakira CD. ✗
9 We **didn't had** breakfast this morning. ✗
10 **Went you** to the cinema last night? ✗
11 We **watch often** cartoons on TV. ✗
12 My sister **can to play** the saxophone. ✗

Hi Julia
How are you? (1) ...... this email from Karen's room at the School of Performing Arts. I (2) ...... send it from my room because I (3) ...... a computer. Karen is one of my friends here. That's her in the photo. We (4) ...... guitar lessons together. She's (5) ...... guitarist in the academy. I prefer singing – it's (6) ...... for me!
On Friday evening, Karen and I (7) ...... to a disco. I (8) ...... a really nice boy. We danced and chatted for ages. I (9) ...... see him again next weekend.
We didn't (10) ...... last night. We stayed in and watched the Robbie Williams concert on TV. Did you (11) ...... it? It was OK, but they (12) ...... his best songs.
Love
Patricia

SONG AND READING FILE

The Beatles

Busted

They might be giants

Avril Lavigne

Are you a product
of birth order?

The growing popularity
of Harajuku

Room for Romance

Life wasn't better
in the past!

With a little help from my friends

1 🎧 Listen and choose the best meaning for the song.

a) His friends help to make life better for him.

b) He's got friends but he still feels worried and sad.

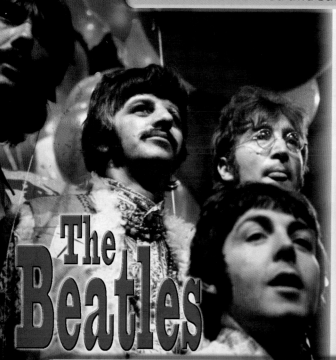

The Beatles

What would you think if I sang out of tune?
Would you stand up and walk out on me?
Lend me your ears and I'll sing you a song
And I'll try not to sing out of key.

Oh, I get by with a little help from my friends.
Mmm, I get high with a little help from my friends.
Oh, gonna try with a little help from my friends.

What do I do when my love is away?
Does it worry you to be alone?
How do I feel by the end of the day?
Are you sad because you're on your own?

Do you need anybody?
I need somebody to love.
Could it be anybody?
I want somebody to love.

Would you believe in a love at first sight?
Yes, I'm certain that it happens all the time.
What do you see when you turn out the light?
I can't tell you, but I know it's mine.

Do you need anybody?
I need somebody to love.
Could it be anybody?
I want somebody to love.

Oh, I get by with a little help from my friends.
Mmm, gonna try with a little help from my friends.
Oh, I get high with a little help from my friends.
Yes, I get by with a little help from my friends,
With a little help from my friends.

2 Find words or phrases in the song that mean:

1 when you see someone or something for the first time:
a...... f...... s......
2 sure: c......
3 very often: a...... t...... t......

> walk out on me = leave me
> lend me your ears = listen to me
> get by = manage to live
> get high = feel good
> gonna = going to

3 Read the Songfile. Answer the questions.

1 Who wrote the song, and when?
2 Who sang the original song?
3 When did the Beatles start?
4 How many number 1 hits did they have?
5 When did they split up?

Songfile

Song facts The song is by John Lennon and Paul McCartney. It's from the album *Sergeant Pepper's Lonely Hearts Club Band* (1967). The Beatles' drummer Ringo Starr sang the original song. There are now more than 100 different versions of this song by different bands and singers!

Artist facts The Beatles started in 1960 in Liverpool. The four members were John Lennon, Paul McCartney, George Harrison and Ringo Starr. They are the most successful group in pop history. They had 17 number 1 hits. The band split up in 1970.

Website www.thebeatles.com

You said no (crash + burn)

1 🎧 **Listen and choose the correct word to complete the song.**

Maybe you need somebody just like me,
Don't turn me down 'cos I've got no car
And I've got no **(1) money/friends**.

I asked you to dance at the **(2) club/disco**
But you said no!
The whole world was watching and laughing
On the day that I crashed and burned
At your feet!

Since the **(3) time/day** you dissed me
I'm feeling so pathetic
'Cos the guys, well, they've ditched me
And it's all because of ...

You and your friends **(4) are/is** laughing at
me now
You think that I'm nothing.
Ask your sister what you're missing!

Maybe that you **(5) think/say** you're too
good for me
(6) Tonight/Tomorrow when you get home
you're gonna see that
I know, I've got something better than you, baby.

2 **Answer the questions.**

1 What happened at the disco? Was it a good or bad experience for the singer?
2 Has the singer got good friends? Give a reason.
3 Look at the last two verses of the song. Who is the singer's girlfriend now?

turn me down = reject me
'cos I've got no car = because I haven't got a car
you dissed me = you rejected me
the guys = my friends
they've ditched me = they aren't my friends now
you're missing = you're not enjoying
baby = friend / boyfriend / girlfriend

3 **Read the Songfile. Are the sentences true or false? Correct the false sentences.**

1 The band's second album is called *Busted*.
2 Matt is the band's guitarist.
3 Their drummer is Charlie.
4 Their first single was in 2002.
5 Their first single reached number 4 in the UK charts.
6 They had two number 1 hits with their first five singles.

Songfile

Song facts	Reached number 1 in the UK charts in June 2003. It's the third single from their first album, *Busted*.
Artist facts	**Members:** Charlie (guitar, drums, vocals), James (guitar) and Matt (bass) **Nationality:** English **First single:** *What I go to school for*, September 2002 **Chart success:** Their first five singles all reached the top 3 of the UK charts. *You said no*, their third single, was their first number 1 hit. Their fifth single, *Crashed the wedding*, also reached number 1.

59

Boss of me

1 🎧 **Listen and complete the song with the words in the box.**

| horizon | question | room | test | life | empty |

They might be giants

Yes, no, maybe.
I don't know.
Can you repeat the (**1**) ...... ?

You're not the boss of me now.
You're not the boss of me now.
You're not the boss of me now, and
    you're not so big!

Life is unfair, so I just stare
At the stain on the wall where
The TV had been,
But ever since we've moved in
It's been (**2**) ....
Why I, why I'm in this (**3**) ...... –
There is no point explaining.

Life is a (**4**) ...... , but I confess
I like this mess
I've made so far.
Grade on a curve and you'll observe
I'm right below the (**5**) ....
Yes, no, maybe, I don't know.
Can you repeat the question?

(**6**) ...... is unfair!

2 **Find words in the song that mean:**

1   say again: r......
2   the opposite of full: e......
3   a lot of untidy and dirty things: m......
4   see, notice: o......

3 **Read the Songfile. Answer the questions.**

1   On which TV programme can you hear the song?
2   Where are the band from?
3   What did they do together at school?
4   Which city did they move to in the 1980s?
5   When was their first album?

Songfile

Song facts The song is the theme tune for the TV programme *Malcolm in the Middle*.

It was the band's second top 20 single in the UK.

Artist facts John Linnell and John Flansburgh are from Massachusetts, USA. They played in a band together at school. Then in the early 1980s they went to New York and started *They might be giants*. Their first album was in 1986. They are very popular in the USA.

Website www.tmbg.com

4 sk8ter boi

① Listen and choose the correct words to complete the song.

Avril Lavigne

② Choose the best summary of the lyrics.

A   You went to a concert with your friends. You liked the guitarist, but he didn't talk to you because he was a star.

B   A boy liked you, but you didn't want him because of his clothes. Now he's a star, but you can't change your mind because I'm with him now!

③ Complete the Songfile with the information in the box.

27th	guitar	single
skateboarding		wrote

He was a (1) **boy/man**, she was a girl.
Can I make it any more obvious?
He was a punk, she did ballet.
What more can I (2) **say/do**?
He wanted her, she'd never tell –
Secretly she wanted him as well.
But all of her friends stuck up their nose –
They had a problem with his (3) **baggy/dirty** clothes.

He was a skater boy. She said, 'See you later boy!'
He wasn't (4) **good/clever** enough for her.
She had a pretty face, but her head was up in space.
She needed to come back down to earth.

Five years from now she sits at home,
Feeding the (5) **baby/dog** – she's all alone.
She turns on TV – guess who she sees?
Skater boy rockin' on MTV.
She calls up her friends. They already know,
And they've all got tickets to see his show.
She tags along, (6) **stands/sits** in the crowd,
Looks up at the man that she turned down.

He was a skater boy. She said, 'See you later boy!'
He wasn't good enough for her.
Now he's a (7) **pop star/superstar**, slamming
on his guitar.
Does your pretty face see what he's worth?

Sorry girl, but you missed out.
Well, tough luck! That boy's mine now.
We are more than just good friends,
This is how the story ends.
Too bad that you (8) **didn't/couldn't** see,
See the man that boy could be.
There is more than meets the eye,
I see the soul that is inside.

He's just a boy, and I'm just a girl.
Can I make it any more obvious?
We are in love. Haven't you heard
How we rock each other's world?

---

stuck up their nose = rejected him
rockin' = playing music
tags along = goes with them
turned down = rejected
slamming on his guitar = playing the guitar very loudly
we rock each other's world = we're in love

Songfile

Song facts	Her second (1) ...... from her first album, *Let Go,* reached number 8 in the UK chart in December 2002.
Artist facts	She was born in Ontario, Canada on (2) ...... September 1984. She taught herself the (3) ...... when she was 12. She (4) ...... her first song when she was 12. Her album, *Let Go,* reached number 1 in the UK chart in September 2002. Her hobbies are (5) ...... and hockey.
Website	www.avril-lavigne.com

Read More!

1 Answer the questions. Tell the class.

1 How many children are in your family?
2 Have you all got similar personalities, or are you all very different?

2 Read the text. Which sentence (a, b or c) contains the main idea?

a) Astrology is a theory about birth and personality: your date of birth has an effect on your personality.

b) Your position among the brothers and sisters in the family has an effect on your personality.

c) Some people are good at talking. They usually like sport, and they're good members of a team.

3 Read the sentences and tick the correct box.

	first or only child	middle child	last child
1 They usually like sport.		✓	
2 They're usually hard-working.			
3 They like new situations.			
4 They don't like new situations.			
5 They're good at talking.			
6 They're often good at music.			
7 They're hardly ever in trouble.			
8 They hate arguing.			
9 They always follow the rules.			
10 They hate rules.			

4 Decide which sentences in exercise 3 are true for you. Is the theory of birth order correct for your personality?

Are you a product of birth order?

Have you got any brothers or sisters?

Are you all very different?

Astrologers believe that your date of birth has an effect on your personality. But astrology isn't the only theory about birth and personality. Another theory says that your position among the brothers and sisters in the family has an effect on your personality. Some people say that it can also influence your intelligence and relationships. Of course, the theory is not always correct because everybody is different. But parts of the descriptions are sometimes true. Are they true for you and your family? Read them and find out!

First-born or only child

You are quiet, hard-working and responsible. You often do well at school and you're hardly ever in trouble. You nearly always follow the rules. You don't really like new situations. People in your group are natural leaders and often become politicians or managing directors. You can be very demanding! Does this sound like you?

Middle child

You are good at talking. In fact, you never stop! You often have a lot of friends. You usually like sport, and you're a good team member. You hate arguing. Don't try to please everybody all the time though! Is this you?

Last-born child

You are often creative. You're often good at drawing and music, but you're sometimes not very good at other school subjects. You hate following rules, and you occasionally play jokes on people. You like being in new situations. The problem is that you get bored very quickly and want life to be fun all the time. Does this sound familiar?

Read More!

1 Look at the photos. Do you like these fashions?

International teen report:

The growing popularity of Harajuku

Have you seen Gwen Stefani perform? How would you describe her style? She has four female dancers dressed like Harajuku girls in her act. But what exactly is Harajuku? Quite simply, it's the coolest place in Tokyo and it is becoming a style brand name all over the world.

These teenagers are in a street called Takeshita Dori, in Tokyo. They aren't wearing school uniforms because it's Sunday. Japanese teenagers go to school from Monday to Saturday and they have to wear a uniform all week. On Sundays, hundreds of young people dress up in unusual clothes and come to a part of town called Harajuku.

Harajuku fashions change every year. This year there are two popular styles for the girls in Harajuku. One is the Halloween style: these girls are wearing black dresses and black lipstick, and their hair is bright pink or orange. The other is the Barbie-doll style: these girls are wearing short skirts, platform shoes, and silver lipstick.

Young people come to Harajuku on Sundays to see, buy and wear new fashions. But of course, music is an important part of their lives too. A lot of young people bring CD players and dance in the streets. Different groups dance to different kinds of music – all at the same time. Rockabilly and punk are very popular. When you walk through Harajuku on a Sunday, the noise is incredible!

2 Read the text. Are these sentences true or false?

Japanese students go to school on Saturdays. *True*

1 Japanese students go to school on Sundays.
2 Japanese students wear school uniform during the week.
3 Takeshita Dori is a street in Tokyo.
4 Young people often wear unusual clothes when they go to Harajuku on Sundays.
5 Young people in Harajuku wear the same clothes every year.
6 Harajuku is a quiet place on a Sunday.

3 Which style are these sentences describing: Halloween or Barbie-doll?

1 They're wearing black dresses.
2 Their hair is blond.
3 They're wearing silver lipstick.
4 They're wearing black lipstick.
5 Their hair is pink.
6 They're wearing platform shoes.

4 Are there any unusual fashions among young people in your country? What do they wear?

1 Look at the photos. Where do you think the boy is?

2 Read the text. Which 'mystery girl' …

a) likes clothes?
b) likes romantic films?
c) likes sport?

The best on the box this week!

Room for Romance

Darren is seventeen and single. His hobbies are sport and films. Darren is this week's contestant on *Room for Romance*. He has to choose one of three 'mystery girls' for a date. Darren can't see or talk to the girls. He has to make his decision just by looking round their bedrooms. And the most embarrassing thing for the three girls is, they have to watch on a TV monitor while he looks round!

The camera follows Darren as he enters the bedroom of Mystery Girl A. It's very tidy. There aren't any clothes, books or CDs on the floor. He can see that this girl tidies her bedroom and makes her bed every day. There are some DVDs on the window-sill, but they're all romantic films.

Mystery Girl B's bedroom is more untidy. There are dirty clothes on the floor, and there's half a pizza under the bed. Darren can see that Mystery Girl B hoovers the carpet maybe once a year. He finds two tracksuits and a basketball. This girl enjoys doing sport.

Darren goes into the final bedroom. What does it tell him about Mystery Girl C's personality? He opens the cupboard and finds thirty or forty different tops and dresses. This girl is the most interested in fashion. Then he finds a doll and two teddy bears. Is this girl younger than the other two, or just really childish?

Now the most difficult part: Darren has to choose a date.

3 Answer the questions.

1 What are Darren's hobbies?
2 What do the girls have to do when Darren is looking round their bedrooms?
3 How often does Girl A tidy her bedroom?
4 How often does Girl B hoover the carpet in her bedroom?
5 How many different tops and dresses has Girl C got?
6 What other things does Darren find in Girl C's cupboard?

4 Do you have programmes like this in your country? Do you like these types of reality shows? What is the best programme on TV at the moment? Which programme do you think is the worst?

Read More!

1 Look at the advertisement. What is the TV programme about?

2 Read the text quickly. Check your answer to exercise 1.

First person:

Life wasn't better in the past!

After three months living in 1900, Katie Richmond tells us why.

As part of a TV programme, Mum, Dad and my three brothers and sisters and I went to live at 30 Sunningdale Road, London, for three months. It wasn't an ordinary house: it was exactly like a house from the year 1900. For example, there was no toilet inside; it was outside at the back. There was a bathroom inside, but we had to carry hot water from the kitchen to fill the bath. There was no electricity, so we used gas lamps and oil lamps for light.

I'll tell you what, housework was a lot more difficult for people in 1900. For example, we did the washing by hand. It took at least a day! Even a simple job like washing the dishes needed more time and energy because we didn't have detergent or instant hot water. At the end of the day, there wasn't much time for relaxation.

THE REAL CHANNEL SEEKS TIME TRAVELLERS A UNIQUE OPPORTUNITY FOR A FAMILY TO LIVE A 1900 LIFESTYLE FOR THREE MONTHS COULD YOUR FAMILY RISE TO THE CHALLENGE?

FOR MORE DETAILS CALL 0171 426 8600 ASK FOR "PAST HOUSE"

Everybody in the family enjoyed the experiment. However, we all had to make sacrifices. My brother Mark who's 9, found life difficult without television or computers. He also hated the food. I'm 17, and I had to share a bedroom with my two 11-year-old twin sisters, Helen and Hazel. I really missed going out for a pizza or watching a DVD with my friends. I couldn't take it in the end: I broke the rules after weeks without a television or a phone. I left the house and made a call from a phone box because I really wanted to know about my favourite soap opera!

3 Answer the questions.

1 How many members of the Richmond family took part in the programme?
2 How long did they live at 30 Sunningdale Road?
3 Why did they use gas lamps and oil lamps?
4 How long did it take to do the washing by hand?
5 Why was washing the dishes difficult?
6 What did Mark miss?
7 Where did Katie sleep?
8 Why did Katie make a telephone call?

4 Imagine life in 1900. What things were better than today? What things were worse?

The British Isles

This map includes all the cities referred to in the Student's Book exercises.

The British Isles

Scotland

Ben Nevis
Ganavan
Inverawe

United Kingdom

Edinburgh

Northern Ireland
Belfast

Isle of Man

Republic of Ireland

Dublin

Bolton
Liverpool
Manchester

Betws-y-Coed

England

Wales

Stratford-Upon-Avon

Gloucester
Luton

Cardiff

Reading
London

Glastonbury

Hastings

Torquay

0   100 km

Channel Islands

Europe

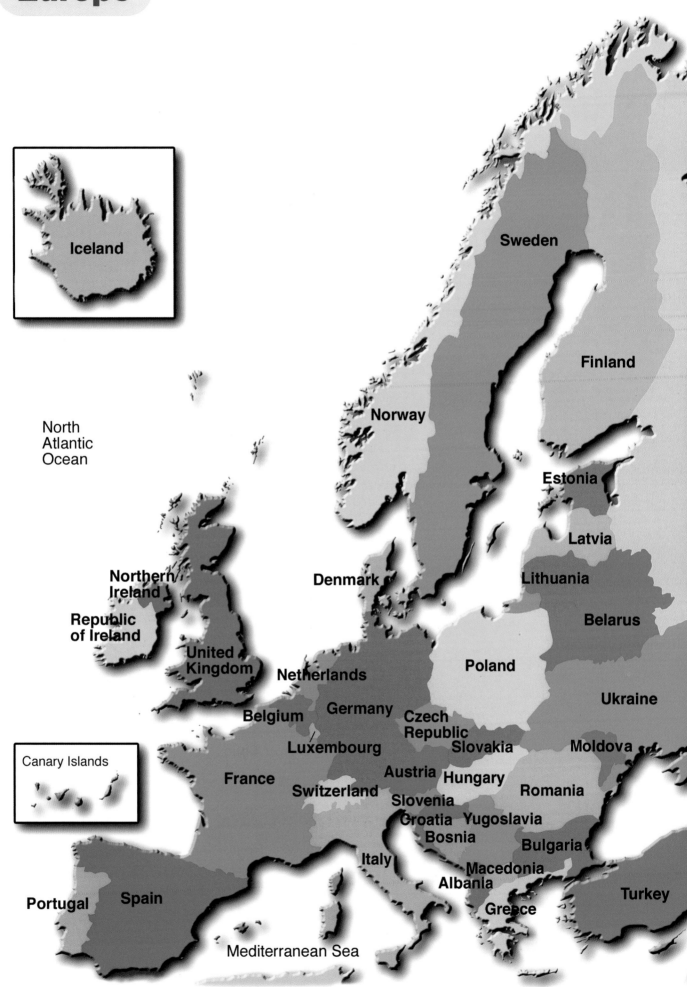

Iceland

North
Atlantic
Ocean

Canary Islands

Sweden

Finland

Norway

Estonia

Latvia

Northern
Ireland

Denmark

Lithuania

Republic
of Ireland

Belarus

United
Kingdom

Poland

Netherlands

Ukraine

Belgium

Germany

Czech
Republic

Luxembourg

Slovakia

Moldova

Austria

Hungary

France

Romania

Switzerland

Slovenia

Croatia

Yugoslavia

Bosnia

Bulgaria

Italy

Macedonia

Albania

Turkey

Portugal

Spain

Greece

Mediterranean Sea

The World

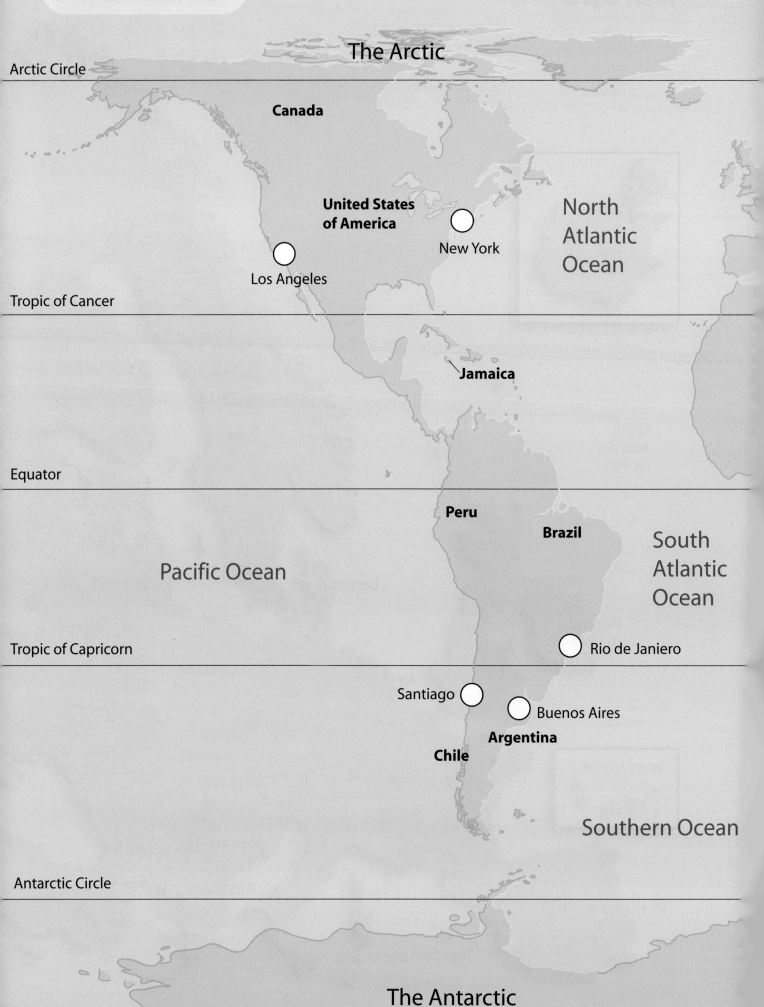

The Arctic

Arctic Circle

Canada

United States
of America

New York

North
Atlantic
Ocean

Los Angeles

Tropic of Cancer

Jamaica

Equator

Peru

Brazil

South
Atlantic
Ocean

Pacific Ocean

Tropic of Capricorn

Rio de Janiero

Santiago

Buenos Aires

Argentina

Chile

Southern Ocean

Antarctic Circle

The Antarctic

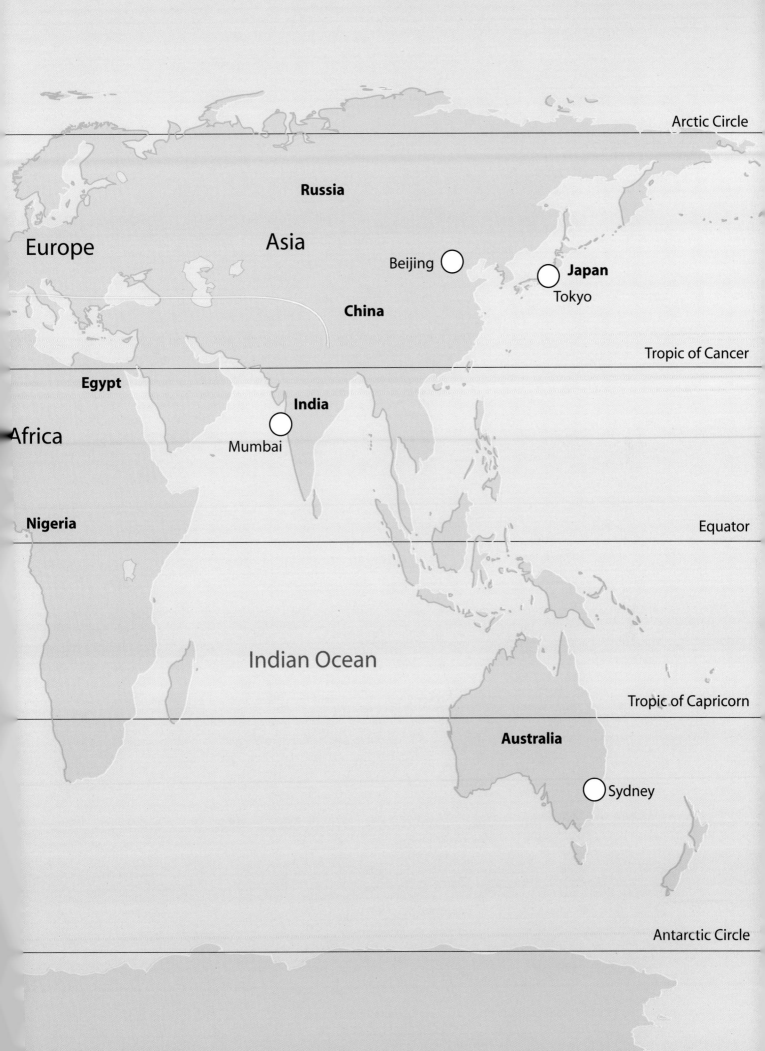

Arctic Circle

Russia

Europe

Asia

Beijing

Japan

Tokyo

China

Tropic of Cancer

Egypt

India

Africa

Mumbai

Nigeria

Equator

Indian Ocean

Tropic of Capricorn

Australia

Sydney

Antarctic Circle

OXFORD

FLASHLIGHT

3

WORKBOOK

Introduction

VOCABULARY

Describing people

→ **Student's Book** ▶ page 5

1 Match the descriptions with the people.

He's medium height. He's got short, dark, curly hair and a moustache.

1 _____

She's medium height. She's got short, straight, fair hair and glasses.

2 _____

She's short. She's got long, straight, dark hair. She's also got glasses.

3 _____

2 Now write descriptions of the other three people.

1 _____
_____
_____

2 _____
_____
_____

3 _____
_____
_____

School subjects

→ **Student's Book** ▶ page 5

3 Complete the school subjects. Use *a*, *e*, *i*, *o* and *u*.

1 _ r t

2 c _ m p _ t _ r
   s t _ d _ _ s

3 _ n g l _ s h

4 F r _ n c h

5 g _ _ g r _ p h y

6 h _ s t _ r y

7 m _ t h s

8 m _ s _ c

9 P _

10 s c _ _ n c _

Food and drink

4 Label the pictures. Use the words in the box.

> apples   beer   chocolate   cheese
> coffee   crisps   lemonade   milk
> orange juice   pizza

1 _____   6 _____
2 _____   7 _____
3 _____   8 _____
4 _____   9 _____
5 _____   10 _____

GRAMMAR

Revision: *be* present simple

→ Student's Book page 5

1 Complete the sentences. Use the affirmative (✔) or negative (✗) of *be*.

1 He _____ good at maths. ✔

2 They _____ from Spain. They're from France. ✗

3 We _____ in the same class at school. ✔

4 I _____ hungry. ✔

5 It _____ very hot today. ✗

6 I _____ 14. I'm 15. ✗

2 Write questions about Alex. Put the words in the correct order.

1 is / nationality / he / what / ?

_____

2 from / he / where's / ?

_____

3 old / how / is / he / ?

_____

4 his / what's / colour / favourite / ?

_____

5 he / what subjects / good at / is / ?

_____

6 favourite / are / who / pop stars / his / ?

_____

3 Look at the chart and write answers to the questions in exercise 2. (Write complete sentences.)

1	Nationality	British
2	From	Liverpool
3	Age	14
4	Favourite colour	Blue
5	Good at	Spanish and geography
6	Favourite pop stars	Enrique Inglesias and Christina Aguilera

1 **He's British.**

2 _____

3 _____

4 _____

5 _____

6 _____

Revision: *have got*

4 Write sentences with *have got*, affirmative or negative.

Mark / fair hair ✓

Mark has got fair hair.

1 we / big house ✗

_____

2 she / blue eyes ✗

_____

3 I / DVD player ✓

_____

4 they / two cousins ✗

_____

5 he / a red bike ✓

_____

5 Complete the questions. then match them with the answers.

1 _____ Maria _____ a computer?

Answer _____

2 _____ you _____ a big car?

Answer _____

3 _____ Paul and Kate _____ dark hair?

Answer _____

4 _____ your dad _____ a beard?

Answer _____

5 _____ your dog _____a name?

Answer _____

a No, I haven't.

b Yes, it has.

c Yes, she has.

d No, he hasn't.

e Yes, they have.

Revision: *there's / there are*

6 Complete the sentences. Use the words in the box.

a any are isn't there's three

1 _____ a bag.

2 There are _____ photos.

3 _____ there any books?

4 There _____ a computer.

5 There aren't _____ CDs.

6 Is there _____ poster on the wall?

7 Look at the picture and write questions and answers. (Remember to use *any* before plural nouns.)

CDs
Are there any CDs?
No, there aren't.

1 a table

_____

_____

2 a computer

_____

_____

3 chairs

_____

_____

4 a bag

_____

_____

5 computer games

_____

_____

6 a TV

_____

_____

7 books

_____

_____

EVERYDAY ENGLISH

Talking about school

→ Student's Book page 7

1 Write the names of the parts of the school.

1 We do PE in the _____ .

2 Teachers prepare their lessons in the
_____ .

3 At break time we play football in the
_____ .

4 We read books in the _____ .

5 We have computer studies in the
_____ .

6 We eat our lunch in the _____ .

7 We have normal lessons in the
_____ .

2 Write the questions for a survey. Put the words in the correct order.

1 at / are / Which / you / school ?

_____

2 you / Which / are / in / class ?

_____

3 are / class / there / in / students / your / How many ?

_____

4 do / do / subjects / What / you ?

_____

5 your / subject / What's / favourite ?

_____

6 does / What time / start / school ?

_____

7 school / finish / does / What time ?

_____

8 you / any / Are / school clubs / member / of / a ?

_____

3 Read the text and complete the survey for Christina.

Hi, my name's Christina. I'm 14 years old and I'm from Liverpool. I'm at Whitecross Secondary School and I'm in class 5E. School starts at quarter past nine. My teacher's name is Mrs Burton. I do seven subjects: French, English, art, science, maths, PE and history. My favourite subject is maths. My best friend is Sally. She's in my class too. There are 32 students in the class. School finishes at four o'clock. I go home after school – I'm not a member of any clubs.

School survey

Name: _____

1 _____

2 _____

3 _____

4 _____

5 _____

6 _____

7 _____

8 _____

1 Good days, bad days

VOCABULARY

Adjectives to describe feelings

→ Student's Book ⟩ page 9

1 Complete the sentences about Sally's day. Use adjectives that describe feelings.

1 Sally was a_____ because she missed her bus.

2 She got 20 out of 20 for her homework. She was very s_____ .

3 She was n_____ before her maths exam.

4 The exam wasn't easy. Sally was c_____ .

5 Sally was really e_____ when there was an accident in the school canteen.

6 She was very e_____ when her boyfriend scored a goal.

7 She was j_____ when her boyfriend danced with another girl at the disco.

8 She watched a horror film in the evening. She was very f_____ .

Word check Places in town

→ Student's Book ⟩ page 11

2 Complete the sentences with places in town.

You can catch a bus at a **bus stop**.

1 You can watch a film at a _____ .

2 You can have a coffee and send an email in an _____ .

3 You can have lessons at _____ .

4 You can buy bread, milk, fruit etc. in a _____ .

5 You can buy stamps and post a letter at the _____ .

6 You can visit lots of different shops in a _____ .

7 You can find lots of books in a _____ .

GRAMMAR

Past simple affirmative (regular verbs)

→ Student's Book pages 12 and 14

1 Write the past simple forms.

1 listen _____

2 chat _____

3 live _____

4 hurry _____

5 stop _____

6 study _____

7 dance _____

8 cook _____

2 Complete the sentences. Use the verbs from exercise 1.

1 Last night they went to the disco and _____ for two hours.

2 My mum _____ Italian at school.

3 When I was born, my parents _____ in London.

4 The bus _____ at the bus stop.

5 We _____ to CDs last night.

6 My dad _____ dinner last night.

7 She was late so she _____ to school.

8 I _____ with my friends at the café.

going to

3 Write questions and answers about Andrea's plans for the weekend.

go to the disco? ✗

Is Andrea going to go to the disco?

No, she isn't.

1 go shopping? ✔

_____

_____

2 watch football on TV? ✗

_____

_____

3 listen to the radio? ✔

_____

_____

4 meet her friends? ✔

_____

_____

5 help her mum? ✗

_____

_____

4 Answer the questions.

1 What are you going to do after school?

_____

_____

2 What are you going to do on Sunday morning?

_____

_____

3 What are you going to do in the next summer holiday?

_____

_____

some and *any*

5 Complete the sentences. Use *some* or *any*.

Have we got **any** chicken?

1 There aren't _____ biscuits in the house.

2 I've got _____ chocolate.

3 Is there _____ milk in the fridge?

4 We haven't got _____ lemonade.

5 Are there _____ carrots in this soup?

6 There are _____ crisps in my bag.

6 Look at Ben's list. Write sentences with *going to*, affirmative or negative, and *some* or *any*.

> *Shopping*
> *milk*
> *carrots*
> *apples*
> *rice*

milk ✔

He's going to buy some milk.

eggs ✗

He isn't going to buy any eggs.

1 biscuits

   _____

2 cheese

   _____

3 pasta

   _____

4 apples

   _____

5 rice

   _____

6 carrots

   _____

must / *mustn't*

7 Complete the rules. Use *must* or *mustn't*.

1 You **mustn't** talk in the library.

2 You _____ show your passport.

3 You _____ smoke.

4 You _____ check in here.

5 You _____ eat or drink when you're using the computer.

6 You _____ swim here.

7 You _____ stop.

8 You _____ run in the corridors.

EVERYDAY ENGLISH

READING AND WRITING

Dialogue

→ Student's Book page 13

1 Complete the conversation. Use the words in the box.

| mind | party | plans | Saturday | some |

TALKING ABOUT PLANS

Damon Have you got any (**1**) _____ for this weekend?

Cathy No, not really. Why?

Damon Jason and I are going to have a (**2**) _____ at my house. Can you come?

Cathy Is it on (**3**) _____ evening?

Damon Yes, that's right.

Cathy Yes, I can come, then. That sounds great.

Damon I'm going to buy (**4**) _____ pizzas and Jason's going to bring his CDs.

Damon Do your mum and dad (**5**) _____ ?

Cathy No, they don't.

Damon Great!

2 Write a dialogue like the one in exercise 1.

Jo _____

Rob _____

Jo _____

_____

Rob _____

Jo _____

Rob _____

Jo _____

_____

Rob _____

Jo _____

Rob _____

Reading

3 Read the text.

A great weekend by Jake

The weekend started really well. On Friday evening, I invited some friends to my house. We chatted and listened to music. Later, my mum cooked pizzas for us.

On Saturday morning, I played computer games with my brother. After lunch my dad, my brother and I watched Arsenal play Chelsea on TV. It was a fantastic match. The score was Arsenal 3 Chelsea 2. In the evening, I danced with a really nice girl at a disco, and we chatted for ages.

On Sunday morning, I stayed at home and helped my mum and dad. I listened to the radio before lunch. In the afternoon, I played basketball in the park with my brother and then I watched DVDs.

It was a fantastic weekend!

4 Put the events in the correct order.

☐ He chatted to a nice girl.

☐ He watched DVDs.

[1] He invited some friends to his house.

☐ He stayed at home.

☐ He played basketball.

☐ He watched football on TV.

☐ He played computer games.

Writing Sequencing words *after, before, later, then*

→ Student's Book ⟩ page 15

5 Underline these words in the text in exercise 3.

> after   before   later   then

6 Choose the correct word.

1 I listened to music after / then breakfast.

2 I helped my mum before / later I tidied my bedroom.

3 I phoned my friend and when / then I played football.

4 Later, / Before we watched TV.

5 I chatted to a nice boy and after / then we danced together.

7 Write a text about a really good weekend. Use the ideas in the box to help you.

> watched a great video/DVD
> watched a fantastic match on TV
> chatted with a really nice boy/girl
> visited an internet cafe
> the weather was fantastic

A great weekend

The weekend started really well. On Friday evening,

_____

_____

On Saturday,

_____

_____

_____

_____

_____

On Sunday,

_____

_____

_____

_____

_____

It was a fantastic weekend!

LEARNING DIARY

1 Complete the chart.

		Yes	No
Vocabulary	I can name four adjectives to describe feelings.		
	I can name four places in town.		
Grammar	I know how to form the past simple affirmative of regular verbs.		
	I know the forms of *going to*		
	I know the meaning of *must/mustn't* and how to use it.		
Speaking	I can talk about plans.		
Writing	I can write four sentences about a good or bad day.		

2 Friends

VOCABULARY

Activities

→ Student's Book page 17

1 Complete the activities with the words in the box.

> cinema   friends   games   Internet
> magazines   music   shopping   volleyball

1 go _____	**5** go to the _____
2 meet _____	**6** play _____
3 listen to _____	**7** read _____
4 play computer _____	**8** surf the _____

2 Look at the pictures. Write a sentence for each day of the week. Use activities from exercise 1.

Monday

Tuesday

Wednesday

Thursday

Friday

Saturday

Sunday

On Monday, they go to the cinema.

1 _____

2 _____

3 _____

4 _____

5 _____

6 _____

Word check Sports

→ Student's Book page 19

3 Write *play*, *go* or *do*.

1 _____ athletics	**5** _____ gymnastics
2 _____ cycling	**6** _____ football
3 _____ volleyball	**7** _____ tennis
4 _____ swimming	**8** _____ surfing

4 Complete the sentences with your own opinions about sport.

1 My favourite sport is _____ . I also like

_____ .

2 I don't like _____

_____ .

GRAMMAR

Present simple

→ Student's Book pages 20 and 22

1 Write sentences using the present simple affirmative.

my friend / read / magazines
My friend reads magazines.

1 Jane / study / art

_____

2 My parents / play / tennis / at the weekend

_____

3 My sister / go / shopping / on Saturdays

_____

4 I / surf / the Internet

_____

5 My dog / watch / TV

_____

2 Complete the text. Use the present simple affirmative or negative.

Craig **lives** (live) in Melbourne, Australia. During the week he **(1)** _____ (go) to school. The school is two kilometres from his house, but Craig **(2)** _____ (not catch) a bus – he **(3)** _____ (walk). He **(4)** _____ (meet) his friends on the way and they **(5)** _____ (chat) about school, music and friends.

Craig's favourite subjects at school are Japanese and sport. He **(6)** _____ (play) football every weekend. His friends **(7)** _____ (not like) Japanese or sport – they **(8)** _____ (prefer) science or geography.

3 Look at the chart. Write questions and short answers.

Name	Weekend activities
Sarah	
Tom	
John	
Emma	

Sara / watch TV
Does Sarah watch TV?
Yes, she does.

1 Sarah and Tom / play tennis

_____

_____

2 Tom / go shopping

_____

_____

3 John / go shopping

_____

_____

4 John and Emma / play tennis

_____

_____

5 Emma / go to the cinema

_____

_____

4 Complete the dialogue. Use the present simple.

Harry What do you usually do at weekends?
Sandra I **(1)** _____ (go) shopping.
Harry Really? What **(2)** ____ you _____ (buy)?
Sandra Clothes.
Harry I go shopping too, but I **(3)** _____ (not buy) clothes. I buy computer games.
Sandra Oh. **(4)** _____ you _____ (play) computer games every weekend?
Harry Yes, I **(5)** _____ . And then on Sundays, I **(6)** _____ (do) my homework.
Sandra Oh, on Sundays, I go to the cinema.

Question words

5 Choose the correct question word. Then write true answers.

1 **Who / Where** does your best friend live?

_____

2 **How often / What** do you go to the cinema?

_____

3 **When / Where** do you usually have lunch – at home or at school?

_____

4 **Why / What** is your favourite sport?

_____

5 **Why / What** do you like your favourite sport?

_____

6 **Who / When** do you go to bed on Friday evenings?

_____

Adverbs of frequency

6 Complete the chart with the words in the box.

| ~~always~~ hardly ever never often sometimes usually |

always	● ● ● ● ● ●
(1)	● ● ● ● ● ○
(2)	● ● ● ● ○ ○
(3)	● ● ● ○ ○ ○
(4)	● ○ ○ ○ ○ ○
(5)	○ ○ ○ ○ ○ ○

Don't forget!

Adverbs of frequency go **before** most verbs in the present simple. They go **after** the verb *be*.

7 Rewrite the sentences with the adverbs of frequency in brackets.

1 I meet friends in town. (often)
   I often meet friends in town.

2 I have eggs for breakfast. (usually)

_____

3 I'm late for school. (never)

_____

4 My favourite football team wins. (hardly ever)

_____

_____

5 I go to bed before 11 o'clock. (sometimes)

_____

6 The weather in my town is good. (always)

_____

8 Make the sentences in exercise 7 true for you.

1 _____

2 _____

3 _____

4 _____

5 _____

6 _____

Object pronouns

9 Complete the sentences. Use the correct object pronoun.

1 My brother goes shopping at weekends and I go with _____ .

2 Shakira is great. I love _____ .

3 I play volleyball with my friends. I meet _____ in the park.

4 We don't like Monday mornings because our teacher always gives _____ a vocabulary test.

5 Listen! I've got something to tell _____ .

6 Listen to _____ when I'm talking to you!

EVERYDAY ENGLISH

Dialogue

→ Student's Book page 21

1 Complete the conversation. Use the sentences in the box.

> Yes, I do. He's fantastic!
> I can't stand Tom Cruise.
> What video is this, Lisa?
> Will Smith and Julia Roberts.

TALKING ABOUT LIKES AND DISLIKES

Martin (1) _____

  Lisa It's a Tom Cruise film.

Martin (2) _____

  Lisa What actors do you like?

Martin (3) _____

  Lisa What about Jackie Chan? Do you like him?

Martin (4) _____

2 Write another conversation like the one in exercise 1. Use different actors.

Ricardo _____

Camila _____

Ricardo _____

Camila _____

Ricardo _____

Camila _____

       _____

Ricardo _____

READING AND WRITING

Reading

3 Read the text and look at the photo. Which girl is Megan?

My classmate

There's a girl in my class called Megan. We always sit together in lessons. She's thirteen years old and she's got two sisters.

Megan has got long, dark hair and brown eyes. She wears glasses and she's quite tall.

At weekends, Megan sometimes goes shopping with me. We usually buy CDs and magazines.

Megan often goes to the cinema too. Her favourite actor is Johnny Depp. She's got five posters of him in her bedroom! She also likes Ben Affleck and Jim Carrey.

4 Correct the sentences.

1 Megan is twelve years old.

  _____

2 She's got short hair.

  _____

3 She goes shopping with her brother.

  _____

4 She hardly ever goes to the cinema.

  _____

5 Her favourite actor is Russell Crowe.

  _____

Writing Capital letters and punctuation

→ Student's Book page 23

5 Write the punctuation marks.

1 apostrophe	
2 comma	
3 exclamation mark	
4 full stop	
5 question mark	

6 Add capital letters and punctuation to the sentences.

1 i sit next to john in my french lessons

2 we go to the cinema in london on sundays

3 johns favourite actor is will smith

4 i prefer english actors

5 do you do your homework on friday saturday or sunday

7 Write about a classmate.

My classmate

There's a _____ in my class called

_____ . We _____ sit together in

_____ . _____

years old and _____ got _____

_____ . _____ has got _____

_____ .

At weekends, _____

_____ .

_____ often _____ too.

_____ favourite _____ is _____

_____ . _____ also likes

_____

LEARNING DIARY

1 Complete the chart.

		Yes	No
Vocabulary	I can name five activities.		
	I can name three sports we use with *play*, three we use with *go*, and three sports we use with *do*.		
Grammar	I know the affirmative, negative and interrogative forms of the present simple.		
	I know where to place adverbs of frequency with (a) most verbs in the present simple (b) the verb *be*.		
	I can name all the subject and object pronouns.		
Pronunciation	I can mark word stress on words of three syllables.		
Speaking	I can ask and talk about likes and dislikes.		
Writing	I can write four sentences about my best friend.		

3 Music

VOCABULARY

Instruments and musicians

→ Student's Book page 25

1 Complete the labels.

1 c _____   2 g _____

3 k _____   4 s _____

 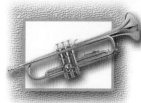

5 v _____   6 t _____

7 p _____   8 d _____

9 b _____

2 Complete the musicians for the instruments in exercise 1. Add -er, -ist or player.

1 cell**ist**

2 guitar_____

3 keyboard_____

4 drumm_____

5 violin_____

6 bass guitar_____

7 saxophon_____

8 pian_____

9 trumpet_____

Word check Clothes

→ Student's Book page 27

3 Label the picture.

1 _____

2 _____   4 _____

3 _____   5 _____

6 _____

GRAMMAR

Present continuous

→ Student's Book > pages 28 and 30 >

1 Complete the sentences with the words in the box. Use the present continuous affirmative.

> get   practise   sit   watch   wear   write

1 Jo _____ a letter to his cousin.

2 'What's that music?'
  'Pete _____ the cello.'

3 The trumpeter _____ next to the saxophonist.

4 Liam _____ a black cap.

5 'Where's John?'
  'He _____ a football match.'

6 Kate's in her bedroom. She _____ dressed.

2 Write negative sentences. Use the present continuous.

1 They / not dance

_____

2 He / not do / his homework

_____

_____

3 I / not wait for / a bus

_____

4 It / not rain

_____

5 You / not have / fun

_____

6 We / not chat / to our friends

_____

_____

7 She / not listen / to me!

_____

3 Look at the picture. Then complete the questions and answers. Use the present continuous.

1 What / Laura / do?

What's Laura _____

She's _____

2 Who / sit / next to Laura?

Who's _____

_____

3 Mark / read a book?

Is _____

_____

4 What / James and Sara / do?

_____

_____

5 Who / buy a ticket?

_____

_____

6 David and Tina / have lunch?

_____

_____

Present continuous with future meaning

4 Look at Harry's diary for next week. Write sentences.

Monday go to the cinema	Thursday meet Carmen for lunch
Tuesday play tennis	Friday go shopping
Wednesday visit my grandad	

1 **On Monday, he's** _____

_____

2 _____

_____

3 _____

_____

4 _____

_____

5 _____

_____

5 Answer the questions.

1 What are you doing this evening?

_____

_____

2 What are you doing tomorrow?

_____

_____

3 What are you doing next Saturday?

_____

_____

should / shouldn't

6 Match the sentences with the pictures. Then complete them with *should* or *shouldn't*.

1 They _____ take an umbrella.   Picture ___

2 They _____ swim in the sea.   Picture ___

3 She _____ buy a new bike.   Picture ___

4 It _____ be on the table.   Picture ___

5 He _____ sing in public.   Picture ___

6 He _____ go to school.   Picture ___

7 Write true sentences.

My best friend should …

_____

_____ .

My best friend shouldn't …

_____

_____

Dialogue

→ Student's Book page 29

1 Complete the conversation with the words in the box.

> don't eating Is she Let's
> She's got 's wearing

DESCRIBING PEOPLE

Christina Do you know Susie?

Kevin No, I (**1**) _____ . Is she here?

Christina Yes, over there. (**2**) _____ long fair hair and she (**3**) _____ a tracksuit top.

Kevin Is she (**4**) _____ a burger?

Christina That's right.

Kevin (**5**) _____ a friend of yours?

Christina Yes, she is. She sometimes plays basketball with us. (**6**) _____ go and talk to her.

2 Write another dialogue like the one in exercise 1.

Luis _____

Mariana _____

Luis _____

_____

_____

Mariana _____

Luis _____

Mariana _____

Luis _____

_____

Reading

3 Look at the photo and read the text.

Street musicians

This is a photo of some street musicians in London. They are playing classical music in front of a shop. The man on the left is wearing trousers and a jumper. He's playing the violin. The man next to him is also playing the violin. He's wearing a shirt and trousers. The man in the middle is a cellist. He's wearing jeans and a jacket. On the right there are two more musicians. The man is playing the viola and the woman is another violinist. They are both wearing jeans.

4 Read the text again. Correct the sentences.

1 The musicians are playing rock music.

_____

2 There are four violinists.

_____

3 The man on the left is wearing a shirt.

_____

4 The man in the middle is playing the violin.

_____

5 Two of the musicians are wearing jeans.

_____

Writing Word order

5 Complete the sentences. Add a subject, a verb or an object from the box.

> him   I   is wearing   she   the piano

1 _____ likes rap music.

2 She _____ a blue dress.

3 Mike's a musician. He plays _____ .

4 Do you like Robbie Williams? No, I can't stand _____ .

5 _____ have got dark hair.

6 Look at the photo. Describe what the people are doing and what they are wearing.

This is a photo of _____

_____ in London. They are

playing music in front of _____ .

    The man on _____

    _____

and _____ .

He's playing _____ .

The boy is sitting _____ .

LEARNING DIARY

1 Complete the chart.

		Yes	No
Vocabulary	I can name five instruments and the musicians who play them.		
	I can say what I am wearing.		
Grammar	I know the present continuous affirmative, negative and interrogative forms of the verb *sing*.		
	I can talk about future arrangements using the present continuous.		
	I know what *can* means and I can use it correctly.		
Pronunciation	I can pronounce *live* and *leave* correctly.		
Speaking	I know how to describe someone's appearance, clothes and say what they are doing.		
Writing	I can write four sentences about a band I like.		

VOCABULARY

Television programmes

→ Student's Book ▶ page 37

1 Write the types of TV programme.

1 uziq hows

_____

2 tronoac

_____

3 prosts ragropmem

_____

4 codmenrutay

_____

5 tileray VT germarmop

_____

6 thac wosh

_____

7 elicop marda

_____

2 Read the descriptions from the TV guide and write the type of programme.

7:05	**Wild World** _This episode looks at tigers in their natural habitat in Asia._ (**1**) _____
8:00	**Daily Bulletin** _All the Important national and international stories; weather._ (**2**) _____
8:15	**Saturday Stadium** _Live football from Manchester._ (**3**) _____
10:05	**The Big Question** _Who can answer the big question and win £1 million?_ (**4**) _____
10:30	**Student House** _The five university students continue their normal daily lives. Which student is going to leave the house this week? You can vote and decide._ (**5**) _____

3 Write your own opinions about types of TV programmes.

I like _____ and _____ .

I don't like _____ or _____ .

Word check Adjectives

→ Student's Book ▶ page 39

4 Write the opposites.

hot **cold**

1 young _____   4 tall _____

2 large _____   5 sad _____

3 difficult _____   6 long _____

GRAMMAR

Comparative adjectives

→ Student's Book pages 40 and 42

1 Look at the comparative forms and write the adjectives.

larger **large**

1 funnier _____   4 bigger _____

2 worse _____   5 longer _____

3 taller _____   6 later _____

2 Look at the pictures and complete the sentences. Use the comparative forms of the adjectives in the box.

good   hot   ~~rich~~   strong   wide   windy

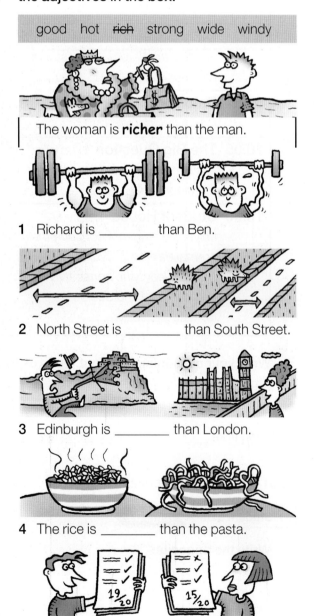

The woman is **richer** than the man.

1 Richard is _____ than Ben.

2 North Street is _____ than South Street.

3 Edinburgh is _____ than London.

4 The rice is _____ than the pasta.

5 Brad's total is _____ than Jane's total.

Don't forget!

We form the comparative of long adjectives with *more* + adjective.

3 Write your own opinions. Use comparative forms of the adjectives.

homework / important / football

Homework is more important than football.

OR

Football is more important than homework.

1 maths / English / difficult

_____

_____

2 reality TV programmes / quiz programmes / interesting

_____

_____

3 football / basketball / exciting

_____

_____

4 David Beckham / Viggo Mortensen / famous

_____

_____

5 spiders / snakes / dangerous

_____

_____

6 Justin Timberlake / Diego Torres / popular

_____

_____

7 Uma Thurman / Jennifer Lopez / beautiful

_____

_____

Superlative adjectives

4 Look at the TVs and answer the questions.

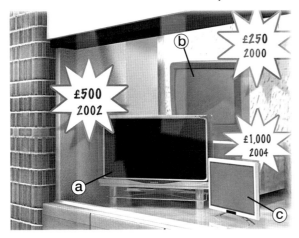

Which TV is the cheapest? **b**

1 Which TV is the widest? _____

2 Which TV is the tallest? _____

3 Which TV is the smallest? _____

4 Which TV is the newest? _____

5 Which TV is the oldest? _____

5 Write the superlative forms of these short adjectives.

1 good _____   4 large _____

2 bad _____   5 hot _____

3 funny _____   6 easy _____

6 Complete the sentences with superlative forms from exercise 5.

1 I love this comedy. I think it's _____ film in the world!

2 August is _____ month. The temperature is often over 35 degrees.

3 Julie is _____ student in our class. She always gets 20/20.

4 The Pacific is _____ ocean in the world.

5 'Do you think English is _____ subject?'

'No, I don't. I think it's difficult.'

6 'Who's _____ singer in your family?'

'My dad. He's terrible!'

7 Complete the questions using the superlative forms. Then choose the correct answers.

Celebrity Quiz

1 Who is _____ (short) of these three people?

a) Avril Lavigne   b) Madonna
c) Melissa Joan Hart (Sabrina)

2 Who is _____ (tall) of the people in question 1?

3 Who is _____ (young) of these three singers?

a) Eminem   b) Beyoncé Knowles
c) Shakira

4 Who is _____ (old) of the singers in question 3.

5 Who is _____ (popular) of these three singers in the USA?

a) Robbie Williams   b) Alejandro Sanz
c) Elton John

Answers: 1 a) 2 b); Avril Lavigne 157 cm; Melissa Joan Hart 160 cm; Madonna 163 cm; 3 b)   4 a); Eminem (born 17.10.1973); Shakira (born 2.2.1977); Beyoncé Knowles (born 4.9.1981); 5 c); Robbie Williams and Alejandro Sanz are not popular in the USA.

EVERYDAY ENGLISH

Dialogue

→ Student's Book page 41

1 Complete the dialogue. Use the phrases in the box.

> But I prefer history.   I don't agree.
> In my opinion,   I think it's interesting.
> What's your favourite school subject?

GIVING OPINIONS

Ryan _____

Jessica Science. _____

Ryan So do I. _____

Jessica Really? Why?

Ryan _____ history is
easier than science.

Jessica _____ I think
history is really difficult.

2 Write another conversation like the one in exercise 1.

Raúl _____
_____

Olivia _____
_____

Raúl _____
_____

Olivia _____

Raúl _____
_____

Olivia _____
_____

READING AND WRITING

Reading

3 Read the text.

Sabrina

Sabrina The Teenage Witch is an American TV programme. It's a comedy about a sixteen-year-old girl. In the programme, she is a witch.

The most important character is Sabrina Spellman. She lives with her two aunts, Hilda and Zelda. They've got a black cat called Salem. Sabrina is a student at Westbridge High School. Her best friend at school is called Harvey. A lot of the other students don't like Sabrina because they think she's strange.

Melissa Joan Hart plays the part of Sabrina. She's got long, blonde hair and blue eyes.

4 Complete the factfile about Sabrina.

Name of programme	Sabrina the Teenage Witch
Type of programme	comedy
1 What it's about	
2 Most important character	
3 Lives with	
4 Best friend at school	
5 Why others don't like her	
6 Name of actress	
7 Description	

Writing *because*

→ **Student's Book** > page 43

5 Join the sentences with *because* and complete them. Use the words in the box.

> cute friend Sunday ~~tired~~ T-shirt

I'm going to bed. I'm …
I'm going to bed because I'm tired.

1 I'm not going to school. It's …

_____

2 She likes my brother. She thinks he's …

_____

_____

3 You're cold. You're wearing a …

_____

_____

4 I like you. You're my best …

_____

6 Look at the factfile and write about Joey from *Friends*.

Joey

_____ is an American TV programme.

It's a _____ about _____

_____ .

One of the main characters _____

_____ . He's an _____ in _____

_____ . Women like him _____

he's _____ . _____ plays

the part of _____ .

He's got _____

_____ .

Factfile

Name / type of programme	Friends / comedy
What it's about	A group of six friends in New York
One of the main characters	Joey Tribbiani
Works	Actor in a TV soap opera
Why women like him	He's cute.
Name of actor	Matt LeBlanc
Description	Short, dark hair and brown eyes

LEARNING DIARY

1 Complete the chart.

		Yes	No
Vocabulary	I can name six types of television programme.		
	I know the opposites of these adjectives: *long, happy, young, difficult*.		
Grammar	I know the comparative form of: *old, hot, funny, good*.		
	I know the superlative form of: *tall, large, wet, bad*.		
Pronunciation	I can pronounce the weak vowel in *better* and *longer* correctly.		
Speaking	I know how to give my opinions on TV programmes and films.		
Writing	I can write four sentences about a TV programme that I like.		

5 People in the past

VOCABULARY

Jobs

→ Student's Book page 45

1 What are the jobs? Label the pictures with the words in the box.

actor	artist	bus driver	composer
hairdresser	mechanic	nurse	
police officer	politician	shop assistant	
secretary	writer		

1 _____

2 _____

3 _____

4 _____

5 _____

6 _____

7 _____

8 _____

9 _____

10 _____

11 _____

12 _____

2 Complete the sentences with the names of famous people. Use *is* or *was*.

1 _____ a writer.

2 _____ a composer.

3 _____ an artist.

4 _____ an actor.

5 _____ a politician.

Word check Places of work

→ Student's Book page 47

3 Complete the sentences.

1 An actor works in a t_____ .

2 A police officer works in a p_____
   s_____ .

3 A hairdresser works in a h_____
   s_____ .

4 A mechanic works in a g_____ .

5 A secretary works in an o_____ .

6 A shop assistant works in a s_____ .

7 A nurse works in a h_____ .

GRAMMAR

Past simple affirmative (irregular verbs)

1 Write the past simple forms of the verbs.

go   t w e n   **went**

1 become   m a b e c e _____
2 eat   t e a _____
3 win   n o w _____
4 sleep   p l e t s _____
5 drink   k a r d n _____
6 make   d a m e _____
7 read   d e a r _____
8 leave   t e f l _____

2 Complete Ricky's diary. Use the past simple of the verbs in brackets.

> **Tuesday February 13th**
>
> The day before Valentine's Day. This
> morning I **(1)** _____ (go) to the card
> shop in town. I **(2)** _____ (find) a card
> for Monica. When I got home, I
> **(3)** _____ (write) the card to Monica.
>
> The next day, I **(4)** _____ (meet)
> Daniel and Monica at the café. We
> **(5)** _____ (have) coffee together.
> When Monica went to the toilet, I
> **(6)** _____ (leave) the card in her bag.
> But was that a good idea? Maybe she
> thinks the card is from Daniel …

3 Write sentences. Change the present simple to the past simple (e.g. *drink* → *drank*).

1 We are in the classroom.

  _____

2 I carry my books in a red bag.

  _____

3 Richard wins nearly every tennis match.

  _____

4 The train stops in Oxford.

  _____

5 I make my bed before breakfast.

  _____

4 Complete the text. Use the past simple form of the regular and irregular verbs in the box.

> be die go have leave live
> marry meet move start write

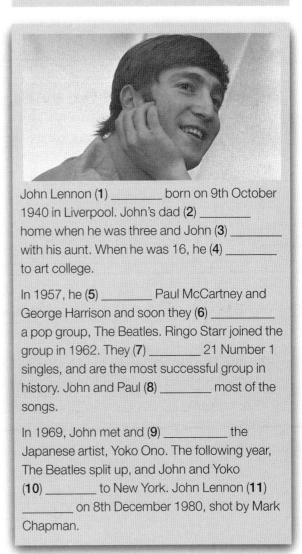

John Lennon **(1)** _____ born on 9th October
1940 in Liverpool. John's dad **(2)** _____
home when he was three and John **(3)** _____
with his aunt. When he was 16, he **(4)** _____
to art college.

In 1957, he **(5)** _____ Paul McCartney and
George Harrison and soon they **(6)** _____
a pop group, The Beatles. Ringo Starr joined the
group in 1962. They **(7)** _____ 21 Number 1
singles, and are the most successful group in
history. John and Paul **(8)** _____ most of the
songs.

In 1969, John met and **(9)** _____ the
Japanese artist, Yoko Ono. The following year,
The Beatles split up, and John and Yoko
(10) _____ to New York. John Lennon **(11)**
_____ on 8th December 1980, shot by Mark
Chapman.

5 Write negative sentences.

We left home at nine o'clock.

We didn't leave home at nine o'clock.

1 They won the match.

_____

2 I played tennis yesterday.

_____

3 She chatted to her friends.

_____

4 Tom wrote a letter yesterday evening.

_____

6 Look at the chart. Write questions and answers about what they did last Saturday.

	morning	afternoon
Maria	🖥	🎾
Alec	📖	🚲
Ana and Martin	🚄	🏖

Maria / watch TV?

Did Maria watch TV? Yes, she did.

1 Alec / play tennis?

_____

_____

2 Ana and Martin / catch a train?

_____

_____

3 Maria / go to the beach?

_____

_____

4 Alec / do his homework?

_____

_____

5 Ana and Martin / go cycling?

_____

_____

could / couldn't

7 Look at the chart. Write sentences about Peter. Use *could*.

	Aged 3	Aged 4	Aged 5
1 swim		✔	
2 play the drums			✔
3 count to ten	✔		
4 read		✔	
5 sing a song	✔		
6 say the alphabet			✔

1 Peter **could swim when he was four**.

2 _____

3 _____

4 _____

5 _____

6 _____

8 Complete the sentences. Use *couldn't* and a verb in the box.

> drink   eat   find   go   hear
> ~~sleep~~   understand   watch

He was tired, but he **couldn't sleep**.

1 I _____ him because I don't speak French.

2 She was worried because she _____ her keys.

3 They were thirsty but they _____ all the milk.

4 I _____ the football match on TV because I had a lot of homework.

5 I _____ the teacher because the class was noisy.

6 I _____ my dinner because I wasn't hungry.

7 John invited me to his party but I _____ .

EVERYDAY ENGLISH

READING AND WRITING

Dialogue

→ Student's Book page 49

1 Complete the conversation with the questions.

> Really?   How was your weekend?
> What about you?   What happened?
> Was it interesting?

TALKING ABOUT YOUR WEEKEND

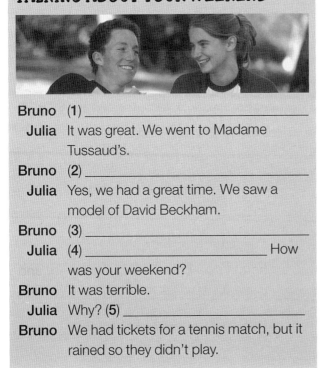

Bruno (1) _____
Julia It was great. We went to Madame Tussaud's.
Bruno (2) _____
Julia Yes, we had a great time. We saw a model of David Beckham.
Bruno (3) _____
Julia (4) _____ How was your weekend?
Bruno It was terrible.
Julia Why? (5) _____
Bruno We had tickets for a tennis match, but it rained so they didn't play.

2 Write a dialogue like the one in exercise 1.

Andrés _____
Patricia _____
_____
Andrés _____
Patricia _____
_____
Andrés _____
Patricia _____
_____
Andrés _____
Patricia _____
Andrés _____
_____

Reading

3 Read the text.

Vincent Van Gogh

The artist Vincent Van Gogh was born in 1853 in the Netherlands. He was a serious boy but he didn't like school. He left when he was fifteen and started work. He bought and sold paintings. He worked in London between 1873 and 1875, and he often visited the art museums there.

In 1877, he started to study theology in Amsterdam but he wasn't very good at it. He started painting in 1880, when he was 26, and moved to Belgium. He usually painted pictures of poor people. The pictures were often very dark. He stayed in Belgium for six years.

4 Read the text again and write the dates.

	Date	Event
1	18____	was born
2	_____	left school
3	_____	moved to London
4	_____	started to study theology
5	_____	started to paint
6	_____	left Belgium

Writing Using notes

→ **Student's Book** page 51

5 Complete the text about the last four years of Van Gogh's life. Use the notes below.

1 1886 – moved to Paris

2 Between 1886 and 1888 – lived with brother

3 February 1888 – moved to south of France

4 became very unhappy

5 December 1888 – had argument with friend Paul Gauguin and cut off ear

6 1889 – went to live in a hospital

7 1890 – left hospital and moved to Auvers, near Paris

8 painted every day but became very unhappy again

9 1890 – died

In 1886, Van Gogh _____

_____

_____

_____

_____

_____

_____

_____

_____

_____

_____

_____

_____

_____

_____

LEARNING DIARY

1 Complete the chart.

		Yes	No
Vocabulary	I can name six jobs.		
	I can name places of work.		
Grammar	I know the past simple forms of these verbs: *find, go, have, make, win*.		
	I know the past simple negative and interrogative forms of the verbs *listen* and *meet*.		
	I can use *could* correctly, and I know the negative form.		
Pronunciation	I can recognise the sound /h/		
Speaking	I know how to say what I did last weekend.		
Writing	I can write two sentences about William Shakespeare and two sentences about Frida Kahlo.		

OXFORD
UNIVERSITY PRESS

Great Clarendon Street, Oxford OX2 6DP

Oxford University Press is a department of the University of Oxford.
It furthers the University's objective of excellence in research, scholarship,
and education by publishing worldwide in

Oxford New York

Auckland Cape Town Dar es Salaam Hong Kong Karachi
Kuala Lumpur Madrid Melbourne Mexico City Nairobi
New Delhi Shanghai Taipei Toronto

With offices in

Argentina Austria Brazil Chile Czech Republic France Greece
Guatemala Hungary Italy Japan Poland Portugal Singapore
South Korea Switzerland Thailand Turkey Ukraine Vietnam

OXFORD and OXFORD ENGLISH are registered trade marks of
Oxford University Press in the UK and in certain other countries

© Oxford University Press 2007

The moral rights of the author have been asserted

Database right Oxford University Press (maker)

First published 2007

2011 2010 2009 2008
10 9 8 7 6 5 4

ISBN: 978 0 19 415312 6

Printed in China

ACKNOWLEDGEMENTS

The authors would like to thank everyone who has helped in the creation
and production of this book, especially the staff of Oxford University Press in
Oxford. We are also very grateful to our project manager, Desmond
O'Sullivan of ELT Publishing Services. Our thanks also go to: Chris King for
photographing the photostory and Helen Reilly of Arnos Design for
managing the illustrations and the researched photography.

Project management by: Desmond O'Sullivan, ELT Publishing Services.

*The publishers and authors would like to thank all the teachers who have contributed to
the development of this course, in particular:* Maria Cristina Koffler, Colegio Juan
Segundo Fernandez; Genoveva Barsanti, Colegio Nuestra Señora del Rosario;
Mariela Elinger, Colegio Nuestra Señora de la Misericordia; Leticia Viarenghi,
Colegio Nuestra Raíces; Adriana Perez, Instituto French; Lilian Berrogain,
Colegio Ramos Mejía; Maria Marta Mora, Instituto Velez Sarfield; Patricia
Mandel, Instituto Smile; Silvia Flores, Colegio Leon XIII.

Illustrations by: Adrian Barclay p. 77, 82, 86 (ex 3); Bruno Drummond pp. 17,
25, 40, 45, 55; Mark Duffin pp. 7, 33 (ex 2), 65, 72 (ex 4), 75, 78, 86 (ex 1), 93;
Richard Duszczak pp. 5, 72 (ex 1); Spike Gerrell pp. 76, 81, 87, 88, 92; Nick
Hawken p. 68-69; Ben Kirchner/Heart p. 54; Kveta/Three in a Box pp. 96, 98;
David Oakley/Arnos Design pp. 66, 67; Kim Smith/Eastwing pp. 33 (ex 7), 35

Commissioned Photography by: Chris King: cover, pp. 4, 8, 10, 11, 13, 18 (Sarah),
21, 23, 26, 27, 29, 38, 39, 41, 46, 47, 49, 64.

*The publishers would like to thank the following for their kind permission to reproduce
photographs and copyright material:*
Actionplus p. 91 (football); Alamy pp. 5 (Asian male), 7 (students), 9 (girl on
phone), 16 (nuclear explosion), 28, 55 (girl on computer), 57 (Japanese girls),
63 (Japanese girls, Japanese crowd), 75 (teen girl), 82, 88, 97 (ex 2), 99 (teens);
Antena 3 Televisión/Globomedia p. 37 (Un Paso Adelante); Aquarius pp. 84
(The Last Samurai), 91 (The Flintstones); Ardea p. 24 (aborigines); Art
Directors/TRIP p. 32 (hip hop); BBC Picture Library pp. 37 (The Bill), 53
(newsreader, Parkinson, The Bill); Bridgeman Art Library Ltd p45 (Simon
Bolivar c.1820, Castro, Gil de/Private Collection); Christie's Images p. 99
(Vincent Van Gogh, Self Portrait without Beard, oil on canvas, 1889); Corbis
pp.51 (Frida Kahlo), 74 (girl on laptop), 89 (café); Empics Ltd p. 31 (Green Day);
The Fremantle Stills Library p. 91 (The Bill); Getty pp. 5 (young man), 9 (boy,
embarrassed girl), 15, 24 (aborigine with didgeridoo), 32 (dancing), 45 (Jorge
Luis Borges), 57 (The Baldwin brothers), 62 (The Baldwin brothers), 94 (ex 1);
Digital Vision p. 91 (bird); Jupiter Images p5 (woman); Katz p. 24 (Uluru);
Kobal Collection p. 94 (Sabrina); Lonely Planet Images p4 (Portobello Market);
OUP pp. 16 (moon exploration), 19 (dumbbell), 37 (tiger), 48 (ex 3), 79; London
Features International p. 31 (Linkin Park); National Portrait Gallery p. 51
(William Shakespeare); Panos Pictures p. 32 (calypso); Photofest p. 43;
Popperfoto p. 45 (Frida Kahlo), 97 (John Lennon); Powerstock/Superstock p.
73; Punchstock pp. 5 (smiling woman), 9 (disappointed girl), 14 (cooking), 16
(worldwide web), 17 (all), 20; Redferns Picture Library p. 45 (Astor Piazzola),
54 (Astor Piazzola), 93 (Eminem); Retna pp. 40 (Penelope Cruz), 44 (Julia
Roberts, Tom Hanks), 48 (Elvis); Rex Features pp. 22, 24 (Sydney, rugby, Kylie
Minogue), 32 (morris dancing, belly dancing), 37 (cartoon, newsreader, quiz,
chat show), 40 (Julia Roberts), 44 (George Lucas), 48 (Charlie Chaplin), 52 (all),
53 (Charlie Brown, Friends, The Weakest Link, Big Brother), 62 (Kylie and
Dannii Minogue, Jack and Kelly Osborne), 63 (Gwen Stefani), 91 (Big Brother,
Will Smith, Who Wants to be a Millionaire?); Ronald Grant Archive pp. 37 (Mr
Bean), 44 (Bollywood poster); Science and Society Picture Library p16 (1950's
television); TVE p. 37 (Cuéntame); Universal Studios p. 42 (Law and Order)

Photography for Topsongs: 93 (The Beatles), 94 (Busted), 95 (They Might be
Giants/J Walaschin), 96 (Avril Lavigne/Jen Lavery), 97 (Justin Timberlake), 98
(Toploader), 99 (Emma Bunton/John Marshall), 100 (Atomic Kitten/Rob Cable),
101 (Dido/John Marshall),

*We are also grateful to those who have given permission to reproduce the following
extracts and adaptations of copyright material:* p 94 *With a Little Help from my Friends*
Words and Music by John Lennon and Paul McCartney, copyright © Northern
Songs/Sony ATV Music Publishing Ltd 1967, reprinted by permission of the
publisher

p 95 *Crash and Burn* Words and Music by John Mclaughlin, Stephen Robson,
James Bourne, Matthew Sargeant, Charles Simpson and Richard Rashman,
Jay, copyright © EMI Music Publishing Ltd, Windswept Music Limited and
Rondor Music Limited, London 2002, reprinted by permission of
International Music Publications Limited, Windswept Music Limited and
Universal Music Publishing. All Rights Reserved.

p 96 *Boss of Me* Words and Music by John Flansburgh and John Linnell,
copyright © Fox Film Music Corporation and New Music Enterprises, USA and
EMI Music Publishing Limited, London 2001, reprinted by permission of
International Music Publications Limited. All Rights Reserved.

p 97 *Sk8er Boi* Words and Music Lauren Christy, David Alspach, Graham
Edwards and Avril Lavigne, copyright © Rainbow Fish Music, Ferry Hill Songs,
Mr Spock Music, Almo-Music Corporation, USA and Warner/Chappell North
America Limited, London, W6 8BS 2002, reprinted by permission of
International Music Publications Limited and Rondor Music (UK) Limited. All
Rights Reserved.

With additional thanks to: Davenant Foundation School, The Globe Theatre,
Windsor Leisure Centre